The Tassajara Recipe Book

"We venerate all the great teachers
and give thanks for this food:
the work of many people
and the suffering of other forms of life."
—Meal chant

May I
together with all beings
enjoy the pure taste
of kind mind joyful mind big mind.

The Tassajara Recipe Book

FAVORITES OF THE GUEST SEASON

Edward Espe Brown

FOREWORD BY ALICE WATERS

SHAMBHALA • Boston & London • 1985

Shambhala Publications, Inc.
Horticultural Hall
300 Massachusetts Avenue
Boston, Massachusetts 02115

9   8   7   6   5   4
Printed in the United States of America on acid-free paper ∞
Distributed in the United States by Random House, Inc., and in Canada by
Random House of Canada Ltd

Library of Congress Cataloging in Publication Data

Brown, Edward Espe.
  The Tassajara recipe book.

  Includes index.
  1. Vegetarian cookery.   2. Cookery—California.
I. Title.
TX837.B863   1985   641.5′636   84-23576
ISBN 0-87773-308-2 (pbk.)
        0-394-73520-X (Random House)

Design/Hazel Bercholz
Typesetting/G&S Typesetters, Inc./Austin, Texas, in Linotron Sabon

I would like to dedicate this book
to two of my teachers:

first of all to my late teacher,
Shunryu Suzuki, who once said to me,
"The most important thing is
to find out what is
the most important thing."
(I'm still chewing on it.)

and secondly, to the Vietnamese monk,
Thich Nhat Hanh
who having lived through untold
suffering, still often remarks,
"Please enjoy your breath,"
and who last summer told me,
"To be happy is most basic,
most fundamental."

Contents

"When you cook,
you are not just working on food,
you are working on yourself,
you are working on others."

Shunryu Suzuki-roshi

Food is not matter
but the heart of matter,
the flesh and blood of
rock and water, earth and sun.

Food is not a commodity
which price can capture,
but exacting effort,
carefully sustained,
the life work of countless
beings.

With this cooking I enter
the heart of matter,
I enter the intimate activity
which makes dreams materialize.

Foreword

My connection with the food at the Zen Monastery at Tassajara initially came through the gardens at Green Gulch, to which I was introduced by a friend living there. The gardeners were interested to know if their produce might suit the needs of Chez Panisse, and on frequent visits to the restaurant they displayed a very lively curiosity about what we were up to in the kitchen. Their energies were captured, guided, and nurtured by the innovative intensive gardening techniques of Alan Chadwick. They brought us wonderful Rose Fir potatoes and baby russets, tender little straight French green beans and all kinds of herbs. I was particularly taken, as always, with the cultivation of these and other disappearing varieties of produce.

The gardens were later expanded to supply Greens restaurant, creating what I believe is the ideal situation for a cook—the garden "right outside the door." I found it very rewarding to help plan Greens' menu, with so many good fresh ingredients readily available.

It's very difficult to bring in supplies to Tassajara, which is located hours above civilization in the Los Padres National Forest, so a garden in the same spirit was put in up there to provide food during the guest season. I've regularly been a happy summer guest at Tassajara and have always found the vegetarian menu delicious and satisfying. I imagine many of us have had the experience of eating stridently "vegetarian" food and feeling somehow punished by dishes most memorable for their meatlessness. But Tassajara food is quite unusual, always remembered for enticing flavors and textures and a special flavor of wholesomeness.

I believe that the best food comes from the simple and thoughtful preparation of excellent ingredients. That's the kind of thing they do at Tassajara, and what this vegetarian cookbook is all about.

Alice Waters
Berkeley
January 1985

AN INVITATION

Guest recipes from Tassajara—I invite you to share these with us. And to share with us the mountains from which they come.

Traveling in the mountains one meets various sights, sounds, smells. Along the way birds, trees, wildflowers, rocks, streams, valleys, and vistas come into view. If you want to see and know the truth of the mountains, let go and make yourself open and receptive. Move with the sense of having arrived each step of the way.

So along with recipes, I give you various sightings, the flesh and blood of mountains walking, because cooking is not just about getting down to business. Beyond business, or in the best of business, is the vastness of the mountains.

Introduction

Tassajara is an isolated, narrow valley at the end of fourteen miles of a dirt road that winds into the mountains. The road passes madrone, buckeye, oak, pine, ferns, brush, manzanita, yucca, and, at the crest along the ridge, looks east to the Salinas Valley, west to the Coast Range. Along here, one can sometimes see the moon rise with the sunset. If not really spectacular, these mountains are rugged and wide-ranging.

News does not always reach here right away. No television, no radios; any newspapers are at least a day old. Big news comes by phone if the phone is working and if somebody hears it ringing and answers it. A single wire strung to trees makes the connection—most of the time.

Tassajara is a Zen Buddhist meditation center, open to visitors in the summer.

The autumn, winter, and spring months are a time of solitude, of retreat, with thirty, perhaps forty residents, and no visitors. Each day seeking the way to live fully, seeking the way to untangle the tangle within and without, seeking how to realize and express the deepest truth in everyday ways.

In summer months, May through Labor Day, we open our gate to visitors, accommodating the public with overnight facilities and three family-style vegetarian meals daily. We cook for about sixty-five guests and fifty students daily. We have been at it for eighteen years.

Guests traveling the long road find themselves remote and distant from the anxieties and turmoil of the daily grind. They can relax and let be, enjoy the sun and water, the swimming pool and swimming hole downstream, the hot baths upstream, and the steam rooms, built right where the sulphur water steam, preheated nature's way and piped through fissures, comes out of the ground. No need here to do, to accomplish, to produce—it is enough to walk, to read, to breathe easily and rest assured, and, of course, to eat.

For our guests we want to cook something special, something delicious, something to dream about. Not everything can be absolutely fabulous, but the most frequent comment—"I ate too much"—indicates that the food is very good. Perhaps the food is that good. Still, the fresh mountain air helps, the hot baths help, and the relative absence of snack foods must help. As an old German saying has it, "Hunger is the best cook," so if you want people to love your food, then take them for a walk in the woods first and skip the peanuts.

What makes food special is what goes into the cooking. What goes into our cooking is generosity more than genius, kindness more than creativity. We labor. What makes food—and everything else—special is the everyday caring, considerate effort. No one works this way for pay. We work this way because we want to make our best effort. Engaging, awakening activity springs up, is summoned, called forth, invited—the guests are waiting.

None of our staff is professional, including the cooks. We do not live and work here to make a living, but to fulfill our lives. We have been drawn to the mountains, drawn to meditation, drawn to a life we create and share together.

The cook's day begins early, long before the sun clears the nearby ridge. Before 5:00 A.M., usually struggling to become vertical, to reach consciousness, to shake off sleep, the cook rises. Light, aside from the stars and moon, is from kerosene lamps and lanterns. Outside, the mountains, trees, rocks appear a shadow world without color. The cool air activates the lungs and draws out sleep. The day, like the people not fully awake, walks in slippers. One's thoughts grow so loud in this stillness; it is like someone speaking right inside your head.

The most striking sound is wood on wood, intermittent, the signal for people to gather, for "meditation," or whatever it is we do, sitting quietly together on black cushions. Breathing. Facing the wall, coming to grips, getting a handle on what it is like to be alive and somewhat awake at 5:00 A.M. Tassajara is a peaceful place, a safe place to unregulate, to "take off the blinders, and unpack the saddlebags," to make oneself at home with whom one is. Settling into the depths. Falling right through the depths. Awakening in the moment. How is it, after all?

While sitting quietly, a cook might visualize how the food was, how it could be, and how to remain composed in the midst of cooking, how to be unfazed, non-frazzled, not fried. Entering a universe of imagined tastes and smells where dreams speak to the tongue, a cook might roam and wander to return at last to the fresh, inspiring taste of mountain air.

The Tassajara Recipe Book

The truth is you're already a cook.
Nobody teaches you anything,
but you can be touched, you can be awakened.
Put down the book and start asking,
"What have we here?"

Though recipes abound, for soups and salads,
breads and entrees, for getting enlightened
and perfecting the moment, still
the unique flavor of Reality
appears in each breath, each bite,
each step, unbounded and undirected.

Each thing just as it is,
What do you make of it?

Breakfast Breads
& Pastries

GETTING STARTED

Washing my hands, preparing to handle food,
I cleanse my mind of same old thinking,
and offer to lend a hand,
freshly doing each task.

Breakfast Breads & Pastries

Most mornings toast will do (and the millet and potato breads will do especially nicely), but sugar and butter are always a big hit for those leisurely mornings spent relaxing and visiting with friends or lingering over the paper. From Grandmother Mary's Coffeecake to the relatively plain Breakfast Bread Pudding, Currant Cream Scones, and Buttermilk Bran Bread, the recipes in this section provide a range of sweetness and richness.

These recipes will take more time than putting some bread in the toaster, but they provide a welcome and generous warmth and brightness. The yeasted coffeecakes, especially, take some extra time for rising, in addition to the time required for preparation and baking.

May we be good enough to take that time for one another.

Grandmother Mary's Coffeecake

Elaine's mother, Gloria, got this recipe from her mother Mary. With a recipe like this, who needs to be inventive? It's a classic, and when you bite into it, you will know why.

The three risings help to develop the flavor and texture, so start early (then go back to bed, or meditation), or plan a late breakfast, but relax—no kneading is required. It also makes—if any is left—terrific toast or French toast.

2 ounces wet or 2 tablespoons
   dry yeast dissolved in ½ cup
   warm water
1 cup milk
1 cup butter
1 cup sugar
1 teaspoon salt
3 eggs, beaten
4½ cups flour
1 teaspoon nutmeg, freshly
   grated
1 cup raisins tossed in ½ cup
   flour

Topping:
¼ cup flour
¼ cup sugar
2½ tablespoons butter
1 tablespoon cinnamon

Makes 2 9-inch loaves
Preheat oven to 350°

Dissolve the yeast in the warm water and set aside.

Heat the milk with the butter until it melts, and then pour into a mixing bowl. Stir in the sugar and salt. (Set aside one tablespoon of the beaten egg to brush on top later.) Once the mixture is warm, not hot, whisk in the eggs (so they aren't scrambled when added).

Test the liquid to make sure it isn't too hot for the yeast—it shouldn't feel hot but slightly warm to the touch, (115° or less)—and then add the dissolved yeast.

Stir in the flour, nutmeg, and floured raisins, beating very well and with vigor for about five minutes to make a smooth, shiny, soft dough.

Turn the dough out into a clean, lightly buttered bowl. Cover the dough with a damp towel, set in a warm place, and let it rise. Clean up and take a break.

After the dough has risen to double in size, about 45 minutes, fold it down with a spoon, turning the bowl as you go. Cover and let it rise again. Take another break.

After the second rising, about 30–40 minutes, turn the dough out onto a floured board and divide it into the number of pieces you want.

Knead each piece briefly and shape into loaves. Place each loaf in a well-buttered pan, making sure the dough comes no more than halfway up the sides because this bread rises a lot. Set aside to rise a third time.

Work the ingredients of the topping together with your fingers to form a paste. When the dough has risen, brush the top with a little beaten egg, make some cuts in the surface, and cover with the topping.

Bake at 350° for about an hour, or until firm and golden brown.

Thanks, Grandmother Mary.

Blueberry Muffins

These are the famed blueberry muffins made by our Tassajara Bread Bakery in San Francisco—"famed" because popular demand will not allow us to remove them from the daily bakery repertoire.

Around Thanksgiving and Christmas, we often replace the blueberries with cranberries, in which case you may want to add a bit more sugar to the muffins. Frozen berries need not be thawed ahead of time.

Note: Though we use some whole wheat flour at Tassajara, our bakery does not use any whole wheat flour in their blueberry muffins—it's all white.

1 cup whole wheat flour
2 cups white flour
1/3 cup white sugar
1/2 teaspoon baking soda
1 tablespoon baking powder
1 teaspoon salt
1/3 cup brown sugar
peel of 1 lemon, grated
1 banana, mashed

3 eggs, beaten
1 1/3 cup buttermilk
1/2 teaspoon vanilla
1/2 cup butter, melted
2 cups blueberries (fresh, frozen, or canned)
1 tablespoon each, cinnamon and sugar (for topping)

Makes 18 2½ inch muffins
Preheat oven to 400°

Line the muffin tin with papers or butter liberally.

Sift the two flours, white sugar, soda, powder, and salt into a bowl and then stir in the brown sugar and lemon peel.

Mash the banana thoroughly and combine it with the eggs, buttermilk, vanilla, and melted butter.

Add the egg mixture to the dry ingredients and stir together with a few quick strokes (about 12–14). The batter will be lumpy and streaked with dry ingredients, but it is essential not to overblend or the muffins will be tough.

Lightly fold in ¾ of the blueberries, again with just a few strokes (5–6). This will complete the mixing, although some unevenness will remain. If the batter is completely smooth, it's overmixed.

Fill the muffin cups ¾ full, put the remaining blueberries on top, and then sprinkle with the cinnamon-sugar topping.

Bake in the center of a preheated 400° oven for 25 minutes, or until a toothpick comes out clean.

If you and your family and friends can't eat 18 of these muffins in one sitting, share them with the neighbors or pass them out at work. You can also freeze them, but how cold.

Anna Beck's Supercakes

Anna and Bob Beck sold Tassajara to Zen Center in 1966. A long-time fan of our cooking, Anna makes her own worthy contribution with this pancake recipe. These pancakes—when made with flours other than white, and with yogurt and cottage cheese in addition to milk—take longer to cook, but the results justify the wait.

2 eggs
1 cup milk
½ cup yogurt
½ cup cottage cheese
½ cup white flour
¼ cup whole wheat flour
¼ cup fine corn meal

2 tablespoons soy flour, lightly
  roasted first
2 tablespoons bran
½ teaspoon salt
½ cup butter
2 tablespoons honey

Makes 24 or more good-size pancakes

Combine the eggs with the milk, yogurt, and cottage cheese.

Sift the dry ingredients together and then fold them into the milk mixture.

Melt the butter with the honey and mix into the batter.

Griddle the batter, cooking about three minutes on the first side before turning.

Currant Cream Scones

Made with all-white flour, these scones are light, tender, and flaky. Made with all-whole wheat pastry flour, they have that nutty, wheaty taste, but are crumbly in texture and a little dry. A blend of flours produces the best characteristics of both: the soft, flaky texture of white flour and the taste of whole wheat. The sweetening is limited to the currants and the little sugar in the glaze brushed on top, the assumption being that, once out of the oven and buttered, these scones will meet with plenty of jam or honey—and plenty of hungry mouths.

2 cups all-purpose flour
½ teaspoon salt
2½ teaspoons baking powder
5 tablespoons butter
½ cup currants
2 eggs
5 tablespoons cream (or half-and-half, or milk)
a few drops of vanilla

Yields 8–10 scones
Preheat oven to 400°

Sift the flour with the salt and baking powder. Mix in the butter with a pastry cutter, or work it in with your fingertips, until it is spread in small lumps throughout the flour.

Separate the currants into the flour/butter mixture.

Beat the eggs, add the cream and vanilla, and set aside 1 tablespoon of this mixture to be used later for a glaze.

Pour the eggs and cream into the flour/butter mixture and lightly toss the ingredients together, first with a fork, then with your hands. Work the dough lightly to bring it together. The dough should have a fairly even consistency; but overworking it will make the scones tough and less flaky.

Knead the dough just a few times on a floured board, then shape it into a circle about ¾ inch thick, patting the edge with the side of your hand to make it smooth.

Mix a little sugar with the leftover egg and cream and brush it over the top.

Cut the circle into 8–10 wedges. Put the wedges on an ungreased baking sheet and bake at 400° for about 15 minutes, or until they are well-puffed and golden brown on top.

It is good to eat when salivating—and if you take the time to say grace before eating these scones, you'll be salivating plenty.

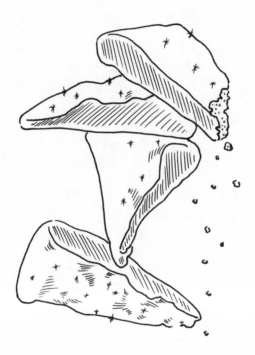

Breakfast Bread Pudding

We serve this often, even in the summer months when the Tassajara mornings can be cool and crisp. It makes a warming breakfast that can be served with milk or light cream and accompanied by fresh fruit: raspberries, strawberries, apricots, peaches. If you have some stale (but not moldy) bread around, here's a good way to use it.

6 cups bread, crusts removed and
  cut into small squares
6 tablespoons melted butter
½ cup golden raisins or currants
3 cups milk
3 eggs
2 tablespoons honey or maple
  syrup (optional)

¼ teaspoon salt
¼ teaspoon nutmeg or cardamon
½ teaspoon cinnamon
1 teaspoon vanilla
2 teaspoons grated orange rind

Serves 4–6
Preheat oven to 350°

Put the cubed bread in a bowl and pour the melted butter over it.

Toss with the raisins, then place in a well-buttered baking dish.

Beat the milk with the eggs, sweetening (if used), salt, spices, vanilla, and orange rind.

Pour the mixture over the bread. If the bread is really spongy and quickly soaks up all the liquid, leaving some bread high and dry, beat up another egg with some milk and add it. Although all the bread cubes need to be soaked, they don't need to be submerged completely.

Cover and bake in a preheated 350° oven for 30 minutes.

Remove the lid and continue baking until the top is browned and the custard set, another 15–20 minutes.

Serve warm.

Variation: This can also be a dessert by adding more sweetening to the milk and egg mixture. After baking, a modest amount of liquor of some kind may be poured over it.

Serve with some whipped cream.

Guest French Toast

Nothing is sacred anymore. French toast used to be French toast. Now it is all jazzed up and we may have to call it California French. Where will it end?

One of our summer guests gave us this recipe and now we can't go back to our old one. If you have some leftover slices of Grandmother Mary's Coffeecake with which to make this recipe, so much the better.

Note: If you do not have orange flower water, omit it. You can, of course, use vanilla extract or other kinds of liquor in place of the sherry.

3 eggs
1/4 cup milk
1 teaspoon orange flower water
  (from the liquor department)
1 tablespoon sherry
1/2 teaspoon nutmeg

1/2 teaspoon cinnamon
grated peel of 1 orange or of 2
  tangerines
pinch salt
6 slices of bread
butter for frying

Makes 6 slices

Beat the eggs well. Then add the liquids, spices, grated peel, and salt.

Let each piece of bread leisurely soak in the batter on both sides, and then fry in butter until golden.

Serve with warm maple syrup or honey, or sprinkled with powdered sugar.

Enjoyable as it is, you'll feel better if you do not stuff yourself.

Butterkuchen

A light and yeasty coffeecake, butterkuchen is tender of crumb and redolent with butter and yeast. The traditionally sweet, coffeecake topping has appeared on many Tassajara breakfast sweets throughout the years. The delicacy of this butterkuchen is so enjoyable, you may want to omit the topping and simply sprinkle a little sugar and cinnamon on top before baking, or serve topped with some fresh berries.

1 cup milk
½ cup sugar
½ teaspoon salt
½ cup butter, in pieces
3 eggs, beaten
1½ teaspoons grated orange peel
1½ packages, or 1 tablespoon
*   dry yeast, dissolved in ¼ cup*
*   warm (less than 115°) water*
3½ cups all-purpose flour

Topping:
4 tablespoons butter
½ cup sliced or ground almonds
1 tablespoon cinnamon, freshly
*   ground*
½ cup brown sugar

Yields 1 large or 2 small
ring coffeecakes
Preheat oven to 375°

Scald the milk with the sugar, salt, and butter pieces, then pour it into the mixing bowl. Let it cool until it is just slightly warm to the touch (115° or less).

Add the beaten eggs, grated orange peel, and dissolved yeast and whisk briefly.

Stir in, cup by cup, the flour, and beat vigorously to obtain a fairly thick but smooth and shiny batter.

Pour it into a buttered and floured 9-inch spring form or molded pan.

Let rise for about 45 minutes. Work all the topping ingredients together with your fingers. After the dough has risen, sprinkle the topping on the cake surface and bake at 375° until brown and firm, about 30 minutes (smaller loaves will bake more quickly than a larger loaf). Serve while warm.

Buttermilk Bran Bread

Thickly sliced and served with ricotta cheese and honey or cream cheese and jam, this bread provides a warming and delicious breakfast. Any leftovers make a satisfying snack food with milk or tea.

1 cup raisins
½ cup boiling water
¾ cup unbleached white flour
½ teaspoon salt
2 teaspoons baking powder
1 teaspoon baking soda
1 cup whole wheat pastry flour

½ cup brown sugar
¼ cup butter
1 cup buttermilk
1 teaspoon vanilla
1 egg, beaten
1 cup bran

Makes one 9-inch loaf
Preheat oven to 350°

Cover the raisins with the boiling water and set aside.

In a mixing bowl, sift together the white flour, salt, baking powder, and baking soda. Stir in the whole wheat pastry flour and brown sugar.

Melt the butter, then combine with the buttermilk, vanilla, and egg. Drain the water from the raisins into the buttermilk mixture, stirring to blend.

Add the liquids to the dry ingredients and stir them together with about 15 quick strokes. The batter will still be a bit lumpy, but avoid overmixing or the bread will be tough. Fold in the bran and the raisins with a few more strokes.

Butter and flour a 9-inch bread pan and scrape the batter into it. Bake in the center of a preheated 350° oven for about 50 minutes, or until the bread is brown and springs back when pressed with a finger. Turn out onto a cooling rack and let stand for at least 10 minutes before slicing.

Relax and take the time to savor the flavor.

If you'd prefer to make these into muffins, fine. They will bake about 10 minutes faster.

Cardamon Lemon Soda Bread

Let the fragrant scent of lemon and cardamon fill your kitchen, fill your morning, clear your head. Here's a mouth-watering giant biscuit that will do just that. Serve warm.

1 cup white flour
1 cup wheat flour
½ teaspoon salt
½ teaspoon baking soda
1½ teaspoons baking powder
1 tablespoon sugar (optional)
½ teaspoon freshly ground cardamon seeds, OR 1 teaspoon already
    ground cardamon
6 tablespoons butter
1 egg
grated peel of 1 lemon
½ cup buttermilk
1 tablespoon melted butter

Makes one 8-inch round loaf
Preheat oven to 375°

Lightly butter an 8-inch round cake or pie pan.

Sift the dry ingredients together in a bowl. Using two knives, a pastry cutter, or your fingers, cut in the butter until it is pea-size.

Combine the egg, lemon peel, and buttermilk, then add to the flour mixture and stir just enough to combine.

Turn the dough onto a floured surface and knead briefly until smooth, a couple of minutes at most.

Shape into a round, place in the buttered pan, then cut a deep cross in the top. Brush with melted butter.

Bake in the center of a preheated 375° oven for 35 minutes, or until golden brown and firm to the touch.

Buttermilk Pancakes

This is our version of a classic pancake.

½ cup whole wheat flour
½ cup unbleached white flour
½ teaspoon salt
½ teaspoon baking soda
1 egg
1 cup buttermilk
3 tablespoons melted butter

Makes about 24 pancakes

Sift the flours with the salt and soda.

Beat the egg slightly and then mix in the buttermilk and melted butter.

Add the liquids to the dry ingredients and stir to combine.

Ladle onto a moderately hot griddle or frying pan and take it from there.

Eggs, Scrambled Tofu & Our Latest Granola

WORKING ON HOW I WORK

I do this chore
not just to get it
out of the way,
but as the way
to make real
kind connected mind.

May I awaken to what
these ingredients offer,
and may I awaken best I can
energy, warmth, imagination,
this offering of heart and hand.

Eggs, Scrambled Tofu & Our Latest Granola

Everybody knows how to cook eggs, right? But we had to learn how to cook eggs for 60–80 people and have them simultaneously ready and hot. Given that requirement, there are no recipes here for poached eggs or fried eggs, because we do not make them. There are a number of recipes for baked eggs, which are wonderfully adaptable to a variety of seasonings and styles of preparation, as well as one for scrambled eggs. We also make omelettes, because we found we could make them on the griddle and then keep them hot and moist in casseroles in the oven.

Eggs cooked slowly with moderate to low heat come out tastier since the protein does not "toughen" as it would with higher or more prolonged heat.

If you cannot face eggs in the morning, the scrambled tofu recipe describes how to make tofu resemble eggs. And the granola recipe does not resemble eggs at all.

Shirred Eggs

These savory eggs may be baked in a muffin tin or in a shallow casserole. These eggs can be quite pretty and the combination with herbs,
cheese, and tomato is flavorful and appetizing.

butter
tomato sauce, ketchup, or hot sauce
eggs
salt & freshly ground pepper
fresh herbs
grated cheese
paprika

Preheat oven to 325°

Butter thoroughly as many depressions in a muffin tin as needed.

Drop a few teaspoons of tomato sauce, ketchup, or hot sauce in the
bottom of each and crack an egg on top, taking care not to break the
yolk.

Lightly salt and pepper.

Cover with a good sprinkling of fresh herbs such as thyme, chervil,
basil, parsley, savory, or chives, singly or in combination. Over that,
mound some grated cheese such as fontina, Jack, or Gruyere, mixed
with some Cheddar or Parmesan.

Dust with a pinch of paprika and bake in a 325° oven for 8–12 minutes, depending on how soft or firm you like your eggs.

Check after 5 minutes to make sure that all the eggs are baking at the
same rate and change the position of the pan if there are hot spots in
the oven.

When they are done to your taste, turn the eggs out with a knife and
serve with toast.

To prepare as a casserole for four:
8 eggs
1½ cups grated cheese
other ingredients as above

Butter or oil generously a shallow baking dish.

Cover the bottom of the casserole with a thin layer of tomato sauce, ketchup, or hot sauce.

Break the eggs into the casserole. Cover with salt, pepper, herbs, cheese, as above.

Bake uncovered in the middle of the oven at 325°. These eggs will take somewhat longer to bake than those in the muffin tin (15–20 minutes altogether). Check after 10 minutes, and turn pan if the eggs are baking unevenly. They are done when the whites have set up but the yolks are still soft.

Mustard & Tarragon Baked Eggs

Baked eggs with cream, mustard, and tarragon are another one of our favorites: fragrant, herbacious, tangy.

⅓ cup cream
Dijon mustard
butter
8–10 eggs
salt & pepper
½ cup grated cheese: Parmesan, Romano, or asiago
1 tablespoon fresh tarragon, minced, OR *1 teaspoon dried tarragon*

> Serves 4
> Preheat oven to 350°

Measure out the cream and add Dijon mustard to taste.

Butter the bottom of a casserole and pour in the cream.

Crack the eggs on top of the cream, being careful not to break the yolks.

Lightly salt and pepper. Spread the grated cheese over the eggs. If using dried tarragon, sprinkle it on with the salt and pepper.

Bake in a 350° oven for 20–25 minutes until the eggs are set. Check after 15 minutes and turn the casserole for even baking, if necessary.

Spread on the fresh tarragon the last few minutes of baking, or use as a garnish.

Mexican Baked Eggs

When we make these for breakfast, we often get requests for the recipe. As you can see, they are a variation on the basic shirred egg recipe.

1 medium-large onion, diced small
2 medium cloves garlic, minced
butter for cooking
⅓ cup canned mild green chilies, diced small or cut in strips
¾ cup canned whole tomatoes (or fresh), drained and chopped
1½ teaspoons cumin seeds, roasted until smoking, then ground in spice
*   grinder or with mortar*
8–9 eggs
salt & pepper
1 cup Jack cheese, grated or cut in strips

Serves 4–6
Preheat oven to 350°

Cook the onions and garlic in butter over medium heat. When the onions are soft, add chilies, tomatoes, and cumin. (Ground cumin can also be used. It can still be roasted in a small fry pan, but not to smoking.)

Oil or butter a shallow casserole. Pour sauce into the bottom. Crack in the eggs, keeping the yolks whole.

Sprinkle with salt and pepper, and top with the cheese.

Bake at 350° for about 20–25 minutes. Check frequently after 15 minutes, turning the dish in the oven if necessary to ensure even baking. The eggs change quickly from not-quite-done to overdone, and they will continue cooking a *little* after you remove them from the oven.

Serve immediately.

White Wine Scrambled Eggs

The alcohol is cooked out when the wine is reduced, but the eggs are still well-flavored. What a surprise the first time you have them.

½ cup white wine
1 clove garlic
8–10 eggs, beaten
½ cup Gruyere cheese, grated
¼ cup chives (or green onions), sliced
½ teaspoon dried marjoram
salt & pepper

Serves 4

Simmer the wine with the garlic until it is reduced to a quarter cup. The garlic can be removed, or minced and added to the eggs.

Beat the eggs and add the reduced wine.

Cook the eggs in butter over a moderate flame, whisking continuously (more or less). With a slow cooking, the eggs will develop a soft, fluffy consistency.

Once the eggs have started to thicken, add the cheese, herbs, salt, and pepper. When the eggs have thickened to a thick mush, stop whisking and let them sit over a slightly heightened flame until they firm up as much as you want.

Well done.

Scrambled Tofu

This is a dish we sometimes serve at guest breakfast, and one which we make regularly for ourselves. It bears some resemblance to scrambled eggs, especially if one adds a little curry powder; this gives the tofu a yellow color. The flavor of the scrambled tofu resembles turkey stuffing, given the thyme, garlic, and diced vegetables. We like it, finding it a quite satisfactory replacement for eggs on occasion.

2 blocks of tofu
1 medium yellow onion, diced
soy oil for frying
1 carrot, diced
1 stalk celery, diced
¼ cup nutritional yeast
2 cloves garlic, pressed
½ teaspoon thyme, crumbled
2 tablespoons soy sauce
salt & pepper

Serves 4–6 people

Drain some of the excess water by placing the tofu on a slanted surface with a slight weight on top of it.

Dice the vegetables.

Once the tofu has drained, crumble it into small pieces.

Sauté the onions in the soy oil in a large skillet.

When the onions are translucent, add the carrots and continue sautéing.

When the carrots are about half-cooked, add the celery, yeast, garlic, thyme, and soy sauce. Continue cooking until the vegetables are as soft as you want them.

Add the crumbled tofu and heat up slowly. (High heat will tend to toughen the tofu and release more excess liquid.)

Season with salt, pepper, and additional soy sauce if needed.

Tassajara Granola

An updated version, this granola is made special by the scent of cinnamon and maple syrup.

4½ cups rolled oats
3 cups coarsely chopped
   almonds
3 cups sunflower seeds
1 cup safflower or soy oil
½ cup malt syrup (or ¼ cup
   honey)
½ cup maple syrup or honey
1 tablespoon vanilla
½ teaspoon almond extract
1½ tablespoons cinnamon,
   freshly ground in a spice mill
   or clean coffee grinder

pinch of ground cloves
1½ teaspoons salt
1 cup (or more!) of any of the
   following fruits, cutting the
   larger varieties into small
   pieces or bite-sized chunks:
   raisins
   currants
   dried apricots, figs, or prunes
   dates

Makes 10–12 cups
Preheat oven to 325°

Put the oats, chopped almonds, and sunflower seeds in a large bowl.

Combine the oil, sweeteners, vanilla, almond extract, spices and salt. Heat this mixture in a saucepan until it becomes watery.

Pour the oil mixture over the dry ingredients, tossing until everything is moistened.

Spread the mixture in a large baking pan or on a cookie sheet.

Bake in the middle of the 325° oven for about 20 minutes, or until the granola turns golden, stirring every 5 minutes so the mixture toasts uniformly.

Transfer to a large bowl or cool baking pan and toss occasionally until the granola is thoroughly cool and dry.

Add the dried fruit and toss to mix.

Store in a tightly covered container.

Yeasted Breads

GIFTS FOR ALL OCCASIONS

Open anytime
A generous, rib-widening breath,
let-go and everywhere all-pervading,
knot-softening, shoulder-dropping.

Open whenever you'd like.
There's more where it comes from.

Open anytime
A most-intimate breath,
with nothing better to do
than touch the saddest most
painful places with tenderness
and warmth, places so long neglected
and hungry for kind attention.

Use often.

Open anytime
A relaxed and settled breath
with nothing better to do
than prepare lettuce and potatoes
to be food for breath.

Yeasted Breads

The instructions for making the yeasted breads are fairly abbreviated, as though you already know how to make bread. If you do not already know how, may I refer you to my *Tassajara Bread Book* (1970). I have been assured by many readers who had never baked bread before that this book enabled them to become successful bread bakers.

Since that time, we have developed a number of recipes—millet bread, potato bread, Heidelberg rye, and cottage cheese dill bread—that have become standards at both our Tassajara Bread Bakery in San Francisco and at Tassajara. The buckwheat, yeasted cheese, and Rieska breads are ones we make on occasion at Tassajara.

One note, mentioned several times since it bears repeating, is not to put the yeast in liquid hotter than 115° because it will not work above that temperature. So the "warm water" in which yeast is dissolved is just slightly warmer than body temperature.

The "egg wash" used to brush on the bread before baking is made by beating an egg with a tablespoon of cold water.

Potato Bread

This is Tassajara white bread—and a quite substantial white bread it is, especially when compared to supermarket squish. A favorite from our bakery in San Francisco, this potato bread makes excellent toast and great sandwiches.

1 tablespoon dry yeast (1½ packages)
1¾ cups warm water
3 tablespoons honey
⅓ cup milk powder
3 cups white flour (unbleached)
1½ cups cooked potatoes, mashed (6–8 ounces potato, uncooked)
2 teaspoons salt
3 tablespoons corn or safflower oil
3–4 cups white flour (unbleached)

Makes 2 loaves

Dissolve the yeast in the water along with the honey. Add the milk powder and the 3 cups unbleached white flour. Beat thoroughly to form a thick batter. Cover and set aside in a warm place and let rise for about 45 minutes.

Cook the potatoes. When they are done boiling, remove them from the water and mash well. (We leave the skins on.)

After the batter has risen, add to it the salt, oil, and mashed potatoes. Mix well to blend.

Fold in 2 or more cups of flour, turning the bowl a quarter turn between folds. When it becomes too thick to handle this way, turn the dough out onto a floured board and begin kneading.

Knead for five minutes or so, adding flour as needed to keep the dough from sticking.

Place the dough in an oiled bowl, cover, and let rise in a warm place until doubled in size, about 50 minutes.

Punch down and let rise again.

Shape the dough into loaves, place in oiled pans, and let rise until doubled. (While the loaves are rising preheat the oven to 350°.) Slit the tops, brush with egg wash (one egg with a tablespoon of water), milk, or butter.

Bake at 350° for one hour or until golden brown on all sides.

Millet Bread

Made with whole millet, this recipe from our Tassajara Bread Bakery in San Francisco makes crunchy, flavorful toast. The millet should soak for several hours beforehand, but I include an alternative.

2 cups whole millet
1¼ cups water for soaking millet
2 tablespoons dry yeast
2 cups warm water
2 tablespoons honey
3½ cups whole wheat flour (or substitute 1 cup white for 1 cup of the whole wheat)
3 tablespoons corn oil
2½ teaspoons salt
2¾–3 cups whole wheat flour

Makes 2 loaves

Soak the millet in the 1¼ cups water for 6–8 hours. (To make this step quicker, soak the millet with very hot tap water to soften the millet sooner. Do not use boiling water—this will make the millet too mushy.)

Stir the yeast into the warm water and add the honey. Stir in the 3½ cups of flour and beat thoroughly to make a smooth, thick batter.

Let the batter rise for 45–50 minutes in a warm place.

Stir in the corn oil, salt, and millet along with any water not absorbed.

Fold in 2–2½ cups of flour, turning the bowl a quarter turn between folds to approximate the action of kneading.

Turn the dough out onto a floured board when it is too thick to handle in the bowl. Knead with the remaining flour, or a little more if necessary, to make a smooth dough. (The millet, though, will keep it from becoming as smooth as it would otherwise.)

Clean and oil the bowl and replace the dough in it, turning the dough over once so that the top is coated with oil. Cover and let rise for about an hour, or until doubled in bulk, in a warm place.

Push down and let rise again for about 45 minutes, or until doubled in bulk. Preheat the oven to 350°.

Shape into loaves and let rise for about 30 minutes in oiled bread pans. Preheat the oven to 350° while the loaves are rising. Brush the top with egg wash (one egg with a tablespoon of water), if you want a shiny, golden brown crust.

Bake for about 1 hour, or until nicely browned on top and bottom.

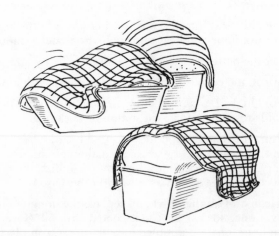

Heidelberg Rye

I do not know what makes rye "Heidelberg," but this rye is light-textured, dark-colored, and half full of rye. Instead of caramel coloring we use cocoa or carob powder to darken it.

1 tablespoon dry yeast (1½ pkg.)
2 cups warm water
⅓ cup molasses
1 tablespoon cocoa or carob
   powder
1½ cups rye flour

1½ cups white flour
2 teaspoons salt
2 tablespoons corn oil
2 tablespoons caraway seeds
1½ cups rye flour
1½–2 cups white flour

Makes 2 loaves

Dissolve the yeast in the warm water and add the molasses. Stir in the cocoa or carob powder along with the initial amounts of rye and white flours. Cover and let rise in a warm place until doubled in size, about 45–50 minutes.

Stir in the salt, corn oil, and caraway seeds. Fold in the rye flour, turning the bowl a quarter turn between folds.

Fold in white flour until the dough is thick enough to turn out onto a floured board.

Knead, adding more white flour as needed, for several minutes until the dough is smooth and resilient. (Rye flour tends to make a dough moist, so do not be surprised if the dough remains wet and slightly stickly even after considerable kneading.) When it is fairly smooth, set the dough in an oiled bowl, cover, and let rise in a warm place until doubled in size, about 50 minutes.

Punch down and let rise again.

Preheat the oven to 350°.

Shape into loaves, place in oiled pans, and let rise to double in size. Brush the top with egg wash or water, and bake at 350° for about an hour or until richly browned and solid on top.

Cottage Cheese Dill Bread

Another of our white breads, this one is lightened with eggs in addition to yeast and beautifully flecked with dill weed. Its lightness makes it an attractive appetizer, and its herbaceous quality makes it good with cheeses, soups, and salads.

1 tablespoon dry yeast (or 1½ packages)
1¾ cups warm water
3 tablespoons honey
2½ cups white flour, unbleached
½ medium yellow onion, diced small

2 eggs, beaten
3 tablespoons corn oil
½ cup cottage cheese
¼ cup dry dill weed
1 tablespoon salt
3½–4½ cups white flour

Makes 2 loaves

To make the sponge starter, first dissolve the yeast in the warm water, along with the honey. Stir in the 2½ cups of unbleached white flour. Beat thoroughly to form a smooth, thick batter. Cover and set aside in a warm place to rise for about 45 minutes or until doubled in bulk.

Sauté the diced onion in a little oil until translucent. Set aside to cool.

Add the cooled onions to the risen starter, along with the eggs, corn oil, cottage cheese, dill weed, and salt. Mix well to blend.

Fold in 3 cups or so of the white flour, turning the bowl a quarter turn between folds. (This approximates the action of kneading.) When the dough is too thick to fold in more flour, turn it out onto a floured board.

Knead the dough for 5 minutes, using flour as necessary to keep the dough from sticking to the board or your hands.

Put the dough in an oiled bowl, cover, and let rise in a warm place until doubled in size, about 40 minutes.

Punch down and let rise again.

Shape into two loaves and place in oiled pans. Let rise to double in size, about 25 minutes.

Brush the top with egg wash and bake in a 350° oven for 50–60 minutes until nicely browned.

Buckwheat Bread

Here is a hearty and aromatic bread. Excellent with soft cheeses or herbed cream cheese, buckwheat bread can also easily be the center of lunch or a light dinner. The loaves will be high and light, although less so if you use some whole wheat flour in place of the white. How satisfying to eat.

1 tablespoon dry yeast
1/4 cup warm water
1 1/2 cups hot tap water
2 tablespoons honey
1/4 cup butter
2 1/2 teaspoons salt
1 cup cooked mashed potatoes, not too wet (about 8 ounces uncooked)

3 cups buckwheat flour
3–4 cups white flour or all-purpose flour (or half whole wheat)
additional flour for kneading
butter for pans

Makes 2 9-inch loaves

Dissolve the yeast in the warm water and set aside.

In a large bowl, combine the 1 1/2 cups hot water with the honey, butter, salt, and cooked potatoes. Mix these ingredients with a whisk. Test to make sure the mixture isn't too hot for the yeast—it shouldn't feel hot, only slightly warm to the touch—and then add the dissolved yeast.

Beat in the buckwheat flour, then fold in the white flour, turning the bowl one quarter turn between folds. When the dough becomes too stiff to use the spoon, turn it out onto a floured board.

Knead for about 10 minutes, incorporating flour as you go, until you have a smooth dough.

Set the dough in a clean bowl that has been buttered or oiled. Pat a little butter over the top.

Cover with a damp cloth and set to rise in a warm place until doubled in bulk, or until a mark is left when you poke your finger in the dough.

Turn out the dough and punch it down. Shape into two loaves and set into two 9-inch bread pans. Let rise again, while preheating the oven to 350°.

With a sharp knife, slash the tops, brush with oil, and bake at 350° for about 1 hour, or until golden brown.

Yeasted Cheese Bread

This bread features cheese grilled into it. Yielding a tender, fragrant, high loaf, this recipe requires no kneading and only one rising, 45 minutes long, so it's fairly quick to make. It can be baked in a ring mold, as a standard loaf, in muffin tins or charlotte molds. This bread is a lovely addition to an otherwise simple supper of light soup, a salad, and fruit (you probably will not want much cheese in the rest of the meal). Any leftovers can provide instant grilled cheese toast or prized croutons for salad.

1½ tablespoons or packages of dry yeast
1 cup warm water
1 cup milk
½ cup butter, cut into pieces
1 teaspoon salt
1 tablespoon sugar
3 eggs, beaten
3½ cups flour
2 cups Gruyere, fontina, or Cheddar cheese, grated and tossed with
   ¼ cup flour
½ cup Parmesan cheese

Yields 1 very large loaf
Preheat oven to 375°

Combine the yeast and warm water and set aside to dissolve.

Scald the milk, then put it into a large bowl. Add the butter, salt, and sugar.

Whisk in the beaten eggs. Check the temperature of the milk-butter-egg mixture; if it isn't too hot for the yeast—just slightly warm to the touch (115° or less)—add the dissolved yeast.

Using a strong whisk or wooden spoon, beat the flour in vigorously to make a smooth, shiny dough.

Thoroughly mix in the cheeses.

Butter or oil a large loaf pan and put in the dough, filling the pan only halfway full. Cover the dough and set it aside to rise for 40 minutes.

Bake at 375° for about 50 minutes, or until the bread is browned. Serve warm.

Consider serving this bread as open-faced sandwiches with herbed cream cheese and tomato slices, garnished with watercress and/or freshly grated black pepper, possibly with some avocado, too.

Rieska Bread

Partly yeasted bread, partly quick bread, this makes a fairly heavy round flavorful with anise, cloves, cinnamon, and mace, as well as barley and rye flours. It's good warm with generous amounts of butter and marmalade.

½ teaspoon dry yeast
¼ cup warm water
1 teaspoon molasses
½ cup white flour
½ cup whole wheat flour
1 cup barley or rye flour, or ½ cup of each (or, another cup of whole wheat flour)
1 teaspoon baking powder
3 teaspoons anise seed

¼ teaspoon ground cloves or 6 whole cloves
½ teaspoon cinnamon or equivalent cinnamon sticks, ground
½ teaspoon mace
grated peel of 1 small orange
¾ cup milk or light cream
2 tablespoons melted butter

Makes 1 loaf
Preheat oven to 400°

Dissolve the yeast in the warm water and add the molasses. Set aside.

Put the flours in a bowl with the baking powder.

Grind the spices in a spice grinder to make a fine powder. Then stir them into the flours along with the orange peel.

Make a well in the center and pour in the milk, melted butter, and dissolved yeast mixture. Stir together until all the ingredients are well combined. Do not mix more than this as it will tend to toughen the dough.

Shape the dough into a circle with your floured hands and pat it smooth on top. Place on a buttered baking sheet.

Prick the top with a fork and then bake in a 400° oven for about 45 minutes, or until nicely browned.

Soups & Stocks

THE HIDDEN PATH: REVEALED AT LAST

Take a look, after all.

Has berating yourself,
being unhappy with yourself and others,
things and events, produced happiness
or unhappiness?

With all this criticism,
blame, hurt, fault-finding,
has improvement taken place?
Do you now, at last,
have every reason
to be happy with yourself?

Leave well enough alone.

Appreciate this carrot, cabbage,
cucumber, and cress, this time
with the less than perfect.
The remarkable flavor you have
searched for is everywhere.

Soups & Stocks

We have always found soups to be particularly satisfying and reassuring, nurturing and sustaining. They are a regular feature of our lunches, along with salads and breads.

The vegetable soups are often enriched with cream, which may, of course, be dispensed with. Lacking cream, the vegetable soups will retain more of their essential and vibrant vegetable flavors. "A cook," one Zen teacher said, "should be able to make an excellent soup using just wild grasses as well as one using butter and cream."

Still, there is something to be said for the addition of butterfat. "The secret of French cooking is butter, butter, and still more butter," a French chef remarked. Have it your way.

A couple of cold soups (other than gazpacho) are included, as well as some long-time standard bean soups and two unusual—cashew and soy vegetable—soups we mostly make for ourselves.

The section concludes with some stock recipes, but I might also point out that there is a simple mushroom stock with the bulgur recipe and a vegetable stock with the Sweet and Sour Cabbage Soup. There are also some marinades in the section on tofu entrees.

Perfection Squash Soup

"Perfection," in this case, refers to a kind of squash, not to the soup. And, although the soup may not be perfect, it is awfully delicious.

We grow these squash at our farm. They have a dark green exterior and a sweet, succulent, fine-grained interior.

Other squash, especially pumpkin and banana squash, could be used. The cream adds a certain richness and softens the flavor of the squash. However, it is not essential to the soup, so can be omitted.

This is not really a summer guest season soup, since the squash comes in later, but we like it so much, we had to include it.

8 cups squash chunks (about 2½ pounds)
2 medium yellow onions, diced or sliced in medium-sized pieces
3 tablespoons butter
4 cloves garlic, pressed
¾ teaspoon salt
½ teaspoon dried thyme
2 tablespoons nutritional yeast
4 cups boiling water
½ cup cream
salt & white pepper
½ teaspoon fresh thyme

Serves 4–6

To prepare the squash chunks, first cut open the squash and remove the seeds. Cut off the skin if it is thick (if it's Perfection squash, the skin must be cut off). Cut into chunks.

Cook the onions on a medium flame in the butter with the garlic, salt, dried thyme, and nutritional yeast.

When the onions are completely soft, add the squash and boiling water, using more water if necessary to cover the squash. Simmer until the squash is soft (about 40 minutes).

Put the soup through a coarse sieve or liquefy in a blender, and return to the pot. Add water if the soup is too thick.

Add the cream and season with salt and white pepper. Add the fresh thyme.

Serve, savor, enjoy.

Note: If you find it difficult to cut open the squash and to remove the skin while the squash is still raw, you can first steam or bake the squash to soften it. Let cool, then remove seeds and skin.

Potato Soup with Caramelized Onions

Simple and soothing, this potato soup is enlivened with well-toasted onions and enriched with cream and buttery croutons.

Note: You will notice two listings for yellow onions. The first, roughly cut, should be stewed with the potatoes. The second, neatly diced, should be fried slowly in butter and oil.

4 cups potatoes (about 1¼–1½ pounds), washed and cut into 1-inch pieces

1 medium yellow onion, roughly cut

2 medium leeks, white part only, halved lengthwise, sliced and washed, OR another medium yellow onion, roughly cut

4 cups water

½ teaspoon salt

2 tablespoons butter

1 tablespoon olive oil

1 large yellow onion, diced

½ cup milk

½ cup cream

fresh chervil or parsley

freshly ground black pepper

about ½ cup small croutons, fried in butter

Yields 8–10 cups

Put the potatoes, roughly cut onions, leeks, water, and salt into a soup pot. Bring to a boil, then reduce the heat and simmer uncovered until the vegetables are completely soft, about 40 minutes.

While the vegetables are simmering, melt 2 tablespoons butter with the olive oil in a heavy skillet and slowly cook the diced onions until they are caramelized a deep brown, about 20 minutes. Stir frequently so they don't burn.

Press the softened vegetables, now finished simmering, through a chinois or sieve, then return them to the soup pot. (Do not use a blender. This makes the potatoes gummy.)

Add the caramelized onions, milk, and cream to the soup. Taste for salt. Thin with more milk or cream if necessary.

Serve the soup with plenty of chopped fresh herbs, coarsely ground pepper, and croutons.

Green Bean Soup with Basil Butter

Green beans, onions, butter, basil—the ingredients are simple, the soup is elixir. Make the basil butter first so it can age a bit.

The basil butter:
1–1½ cups basil leaves, chopped
5 tablespoons softened butter
zest of one lemon (or peel thinly with vegetable peeler and mince finely)
juice of one lemon
¼ teaspoon salt

Pound the chopped basil leaves in a mortar with the salt to release their flavor.

Mix together with the butter, lemon zest, juice, and salt.

Cover and set aside to develop in flavor while making the soup.

Leftover basil butter can be used with cooked vegetables, potatoes, pasta, or as a spread on bread.

The soup:
1 medium yellow onion, sliced or diced
½ cup scallions (including 4–5 inches of the green tops), chopped
4 tablespoons butter
1 teaspoon salt
2 pounds green beans, tipped and sectioned (about inch-long)
2 quarts vegetable stock or water
½–1 cup cream (optional)
salt & freshly ground black pepper

Serves 6–8

Fry the onions and scallions in the melted butter over moderate heat. After several minutes, add the salt and continue cooking until they are completely soft. Set aside.

Cook the beans in boiling, lightly salted water until they are bright green and tender. Drain them in a colander set over a pot so you can save the water for the soup.

In a soup pot, combine the cooked onions and beans with 6 cups of the cooking water (make sure it's not too salty before you use it), vegetable stock, or fresh water. Bring to a boil, reduce the heat, and simmer for 15 minutes.

Purée the soup in a blender, or pass it through either a chinois or a fine sieve. Return the soup to the soup pot, add the cream and more water or stock as necessary to bring the soup to the consistency you want.

Taste for salt. Serve each bowl with a spoonful of basil butter and a grinding of pepper.

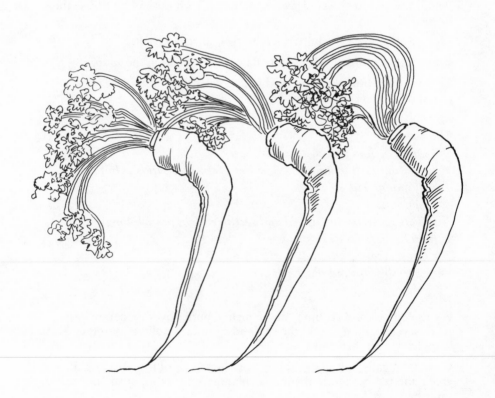

Carrot Soup with Orange

There is a certain mystery to this soup: it's not so obvious that it is made of carrot. The orange flavor sneaks in with the carrot to produce a subtle combination of flavors. (Note: When cooking with acidic items such as orange, use a non-aluminum pot which won't react with the acid.)

Now you know the secret, try the soup.

3 tablespoons butter
½ yellow onion, sliced or diced
white of a leek, coarsely chopped, OR use another ½ onion if no leek is available
1 pound carrots, peeled and sliced
1 teaspoon salt
1 teaspoon nutritional yeast (optional)

¼ cup fresh parsley, minced
1 bay leaf
1 teaspoon fresh thyme, minced
8 cups water
peel of ½ orange, finely minced
juice of one orange
¼ cup cream
chervil or parsley (for garnish), minced
white pepper, freshly ground

Makes about 8 cups

Melt the butter in a (non-aluminum) stock pot over moderate heat. Add the onions and leeks and cook, stirring, for 5 minutes.

Add the carrots and salt, stir to combine, and cook 10 minutes more.

Add the nutritional yeast (if you are using it) and stir another few minutes.

Add the herbs and the water and bring to a boil. Reduce the heat to maintain a slow bubbling and cook 25 minutes.

Remove the soup from the heat, liquify in a blender until smooth, then strain through a fine sieve back into the pot.

Return the soup to the stove and add the orange peel, orange juice, and cream, stirring over low heat to combine.

Taste for salt. When the soup is hot, turn off the heat, cover and let stand for 15 minutes to allow the flavors to develop.

If necessary, reheat to serve. Garnish with fresh herbs and a twist of white pepper.

Sweet and Sour Cabbage Soup

This is a fragrant and pleasing soup, light enough to be enjoyed in the heat of the summer, yet hearty enough for cooler times as well. The stock provides much of the intensity and complexity of flavors. Start the stock first and while it is simmering you can work on the soup.

For the vegetable stock:
1 onion, peeled and quartered
trimmings from the cabbage used
  in the soup
2 bay leaves
1 carrot, peeled and sliced
2 stalks celery or fennel, sliced

4 sprigs thyme
1 teaspoon fennel seed
1 teaspoon dill seed
½ teaspoon coriander seed
1 teaspoon salt
10 cups water

Makes about 8 cups

Combine all the ingredients in a stock pot. Bring to a boil and then simmer for 25–30 minutes. Strain.

For the soup:
2 tablespoons butter
1 yellow onion, diced
1 small potato, cut into small
  cubes (¼–½ inches)
1 stalk celery, thinly sliced or
  diced, OR 3–4 stalks fennel,
  finely sliced
1 carrot, sliced into thin rounds
  or small matchsticks, or diced
½ teaspoon salt
2 teaspoons dill seed
1 teaspoon fennel seed
1 teaspoon coriander seed,
  pulverized with mortar and
  pestle

3 cups green cabbage, chopped
  into bite-sized pieces
4 large ripe tomatoes, peeled and
  chunked, OR 2½ cups chopped
  canned tomatoes (juice
  reserved)
8 cups vegetable stock
2–3 tablespoons rice wine or
  cider vinegar
2–3 tablespoons brown sugar
fresh ground pepper
fresh dill or fennel (for garnish),
  minced
sour cream (optional)

Makes 12–14 cups

Melt the butter in a large, non-aluminum (if possible) stock pot. Add the onions and cook them over moderate heat until transparent.

Add the potatoes, celery or fennel, carrots, salt, and herbs. Cook for 15 minutes, stirring occasionally.

Add the cabbage, tomatoes, and reserved juice. Simmer for 5 minutes.

Add the 8 cups vegetable stock, bring to boil, and then reduce to simmer for 30 minutes.

Taste for salt. Add the vinegar and sugar, starting with the smaller amounts and adding more of each as needed to balance or enlarge the tartness.

Simmer a few more minutes.

Serve garnished with black pepper and plenty of the fresh dill or fennel, or with sour cream.

Spinach or Chard Soup

How wonderful can spinach or chard taste? Make this soup and find out. You cannot see the cheese when the soup is finished, but it adds a depth or "meatiness" to the flavor. The soup is blended, so the stems can be left on the spinach or chard. Although most any cheese will go well in this soup, stay away from the most stringy, like mozzarella. Some Parmesan, asiago, or Romano makes an especially welcome addition.

*1½–2 gallons fresh spinach or chard, washed, and lightly pressed into
   measuring cup*
2 small yellow onions, sliced or diced
1 tablespoon soy oil
½ teaspoon salt
2 medium cloves of garlic, pressed or minced
3 tablespoons nutritional yeast
2 cups vegetable stock or water, boiling
½–1 cup cheese scraps, hunks, pieces, or slabs, grated
salt & white pepper
fresh basil (optional)

Makes 8–10 cups

Wash the spinach or chard very well, making sure no grit remains. (This usually requires a couple of rinsings.) Although you needn't de-stem the spinach or chard, cut it crosswise in 1-inch strips.

Sauté the onions in the soy oil for a few minutes until they turn translucent. Add the salt, garlic, and nutritional yeast, and continue cooking another 5 minutes.

Add the greens and cover to steam them until they are wilted, stirring occasionally.

Add the boiling stock or water, and simmer until the greens are soft, including the stalks.

With a blender, blend the soup to an even consistency, return to the stove. Add the grated cheese. (We use up a lot of odds and ends of cheese with this recipe—all those dried-up edges or older ends can be grated into the soup.) Use more cheese if it is mild, less if it is sharp.

Season with salt and white pepper. Fresh basil makes an excellent garnish.

58

Lentil Tomato Mint Soup

Lentils can be seasoned any number of ways, and this lentil soup, flavored with tomato and mint, has a delightfully fresh taste.

1½ cups lentils
8 cups water or stock (unsalted)
bay leaf
½ teaspoon thyme
¼ teaspoon sage
1 large red onion, diced
butter
olive oil
2–3 stalks celery, sliced

2–3 cloves of garlic, minced or pressed
4 medium to large tomatoes, blanched and peeled, OR a 1-pound tin of canned tomatoes, drained
2–2½ tablespoons fresh mint, minced
salt & pepper

Makes about 10 cups

Cook the lentils in the water or stock along with the bay leaf, thyme, and sage for about 2 hours until the lentils are well-softened. (Or, pressure cook for 15 minutes).

Sauté the red onion in a little butter and olive oil for a few minutes before adding the celery and garlic. Continue sautéing until the celery softens a bit.

Chunk the tomatoes and add them to the vegetables. Simmer for 10 minutes and then remove from the heat.

Add the vegetables to the softened lentils.

Season with the mint, salt, and pepper, and simmer until serving time. Check the seasoning.

Kale & White Bean Soup

Substantial and warming, this soup is especially good when the weather is cool. The assertive strength of the kale contrasts with the creaminess of the beans. Other strong greens—such as mustard, collards, or sorrel—would also work well. Spinach and chard tend to be too sweet for this soup.

1½ cups navy beans, cleaned
   and sorted, soaked overnight
3 quarts water
1 bay leaf
3–4 sage leaves, fresh or dried
2 large cloves garlic, peeled
2 tablespoons butter
1½ cups finely diced yellow
   onions

1 tablespoon nutritional yeast
1 teaspoon salt
freshly ground pepper
6–8 cups kale, stemmed and
   chopped to spoon size
cream to finish (optional)

Yields 8–10 cups

Simmer the beans in 3 quarts of water with the bay leaf, sage, and whole garlic cloves until the beans are completely soft, about 2–2½ hours.

Remove one quarter of the cooked beans, purée them in a food mill or blender, then return them to the pot. The puree will give the soup a creamy background texture.

Heat 1 tablespoon butter in a skillet, add the onions, then cook until transparent. When soft, add the yeast, a teaspoon of salt, and several grindings of pepper. Stir frequently to prevent the yeast from sticking to the pan. Cook for 5 minutes then add the mixture to the cooked beans.

Cook the kale in the remaining butter until it is wilted. Combine with the beans and add enough water to bring the volume to about 3 quarts. Bring to a boil and simmer for 1 hour.

Check the seasonings and finish the soup with cream, if desired.

Enjoy with some dark bread and a cabbage salad.

Chickpea & Spinach Soup

Spicy with garlic, chili, and thyme; earthy with chickpeas; tart with spinach; sweet with onions and tomato—this soup has a lot of flavor interest. The ancho chili called for is a large, mild chili with a sweetness reminiscent of prunes. They are occasionally available in large supermarkets and specialty shops, as well as in Mexican markets.

1½ cups dry chickpeas
  (garbanzo beans)
1 medium red onion, diced small
1½ teaspoons fresh thyme leaves,
  coarsely minced, OR ½
  teaspoon dried thyme
3–4 tablespoons olive oil
3 cloves of garlic, minced
1 ancho chili, toasted and
  ground, OR ¼ teaspoon chili
  powder, OR 1 teaspoon
  paprika
4 large tomatoes, very ripe,

peeled, seeded, and chopped,
  OR 2 cups canned tomatoes,
  chopped (juice reserved)
1 bay leaf
1 teaspoon salt
⅓ cup sherry
8 cups cooking liquid, from the
  chickpeas, a vegetable stock,
  or juice from canned tomatoes
1 bunch spinach, stems removed
  and leaves finely chopped
salt & freshly grated black
  pepper

Makes about 12 cups of soup

Soak the chickpeas overnight. Cook them with at least 4 cups of water for 3 hours or more until soft (or pressure cook for 20–30 minutes). Be sure *not* to put in any salt until later, after the beans are soft.

Cook the onions and thyme in the olive oil over a medium flame until the onion is soft.

Increase the heat and add the garlic, chili (or paprika), tomatoes, bay leaf, salt, and sherry. Stew for 15 minutes.

Add the cooked chickpeas and the 8 cups of liquid—from the chickpeas, the canned tomatoes, stock, or water. Simmer for 20–30 minutes to let the beans absorb some of the flavors.

Add the spinach leaves (cut small enough so that they don't dangle out of the spoon when eating) and cook 5 minutes more.

Check for salt and add pepper to taste.

Yellow Pea with Cumin & Lemon

The earthy flavor of the peas in this soup is accented with a pronounced lemon flavor and spiced with cumin. Reassuring yet stimulating.

2 cups yellow split peas, sorted and rinsed
8 cups water
1 bay leaf
2 tablespoons butter
1 tablespoon olive oil
1 red or yellow onion, finely chopped
1 small carrot, peeled and finely diced
2 stalks celery, finely diced or thinly sliced

2 cloves garlic, minced
½ teaspoon salt
3–4 teaspoons cumin seeds, ground in a spice mill
grated peel and juice of 1–2 lemons
fresh ground black pepper
paprika
fresh parsley or cilantro, minced, for garnish

Yields about 8 cups

Bring the peas, water, and bay leaf to a boil. Then simmer until the peas are completely soft, about 45 minutes.

Press through a chinois or sieve and return the purée to the soup pot.

Melt the butter and olive oil in a skillet over medium heat.

Add the onions and cook until soft. Add the carrot, celery, garlic, salt, and ground cumin and cook 10 minutes.

Add the vegetables to the pea purée and simmer until they are soft. (Rinse out the skillet with a small amount of water, then add the water to the soup.) Add lemon peel and juice to taste.

Check for salt and cumin and add more of each if desired.

Finish with black pepper to taste and serve sprinkled with paprika and garnished with the fresh herbs.

Try it with Cottage Cheese Dill Bread and a Chinese cabbage salad.

Fruit Soup

This is one of the most requested recipes of the guest season. At midday in the hot, dry Tassajara Valley, cold fruit soup is deliciously refreshing, always a pleasure. A variety of fruit juices and puréed fruits make up the base with cut fruit added to bob and float, and appear at the bottom. Simple . . . and the possibilities are endless, so experiment with what's in season, what's on hand, and what's on mind.

Stock:
1 cup cranberry juice
1 cup apple juice
½ cup orange juice
½ cup coarse-cut seeded
    watermelon, blended
½ cup strawberries, blended
½ cup coarse-cut peaches,
    blended
1 cup bananas, blended
⅜ cup lemon or lime juice

Optional:
¼–½ cup white or red wine,
    sake, or champagne
fresh mint leaves, blended in
    with the fruit
¼ teaspoon cinnamon
⅛ teaspoon cardamon

Cut fruit:
½ cup strawberry halves
½ cup watermelon chunks
½ cup seedless grapes
½ cup peach slices, halved

½ cup pineapple chunks
½ cup cantaloupe balls or
    chunks
½ cup honeydew balls or chunks

Makes about 8 cups

Combine stock ingredients for the liquid base, adding optional ingredients to taste. If possible, start early, as the flavors improve as the concoction sits.

Add the cut fruit.

After making melon balls, any melon remnants that remain can also be puréed.

Yogurt Soup with Garden Herbs & Flowers

This summer soup is gorgeous and refreshingly cool and crunchy. Your home herb garden comes in handy here, and you can appreciate having labored to tend it. Now you can relax and enjoy the bounty with some Heidelberg Rye and some Chinese Cabbage with Orange and Tahini Dressing.

2 cups (a pint) yogurt
1 cup milk
1 cup buttermilk or cream
1½ tablespoons olive oil
1 teaspoon salt
1 teaspoon white wine vinegar
sugar to taste (or honey)
1 cucumber, peeled, seeded, an⟨
   grated, or diced small
2½ tablespoons minced gherki⟨

¼ cup chives, sliced into thin
   rounds (save some for garnish)
½ cup or more herbs—
   marjoram, basil, thyme,
   hyssop, summer savory—from
   the garden, minced
1 tablespoon mint, minced
freshly ground black pepper
herb blossoms—chive, thyme, or
   hyssop flowers—for garnish

Serves 4–6

Whisk the yogurt in a bowl until smooth. Add the milk and buttermilk (or cream), olive oil, salt, and vinegar. Stir well.

Taste for tartness and add sugar (or honey) to taste. (Don't make it like a dessert, though.)

Add the cucumber, gherkins, chives, mixed herbs, and mint. Cover and chill for at least one hour to allow the flavors to mature.

Serve garnished with pepper and a scattering of the tiny herb blossoms and chives.

Soy Vegetable Soup

Here is a cream soup recipe made with soy milk instead of dairy milk. Delicately flavored with a lighter feeling than ordinary cream soups, it is nonetheless nourishing and satisfying. Not often served in the summer, we frequently make it for ourselves in the winter months.

2 medium carrots, grated or matchsticks
3 stalks celery, thinly sliced
oil for sautéing
3 tablespoons soy oil
¼ cup whole wheat pastry flour
7 cups soy milk, hot, but not boiling
2 teaspoons soy sauce
salt & pepper
scallions or chives, for garnish

Makes 2 quarts

Sauté the vegetables until they are soft.

Heat the soy oil in a saucepan and add the flour to make a roux. Cook 4–5 minutes to toast the flour so that it has a nutty flavor. Whisk in the heated soy milk. Do not boil the soup after this. Keep it on low heat.

Add the sautéed vegetables and the soy sauce. Do not add more than the 2 teaspoons of soy sauce or the soup will curdle. Season with salt and pepper.

Sliced scallions or chives make an excellent garnish.

A quick, simple, satisfying soup—you're ready to eat.

Cashew Soup

When people stop eating meat, they start coming up with some unusual concoctions. Here is one such concoction—a soup that is very rich (in oil) and fairly expensive, too (though meat can also be costly). Not for everyone's taste, but those who like it, love it. It is one of our regulars for cold winter morning breakfasts.

3½ cups cashews
1 small clove garlic, minced finely
sesame or other oil for sautéing
1 cup milk
4–5 cups water, boiling
1 tablespoon soy sauce
salt to taste
pinch(es) cardamon
pinch(es) cayenne

Serves 4–6

Roast the cashews in a frying pan over moderate heat, stirring to prevent burning, until their bouquet fills the room. Grind the nuts finely in a hand mill or blender.

Sauté the garlic briefly in the sesame oil in a saucepan. Then add the cashew meal and continue cooking over moderate heat for 5 minutes.

Combine the milk and water and gradually add it to the nutmeal, whisking to prevent lumping.

Simmer over moderate heat and add the seasonings to taste. Add the soy sauce before adding the salt so you do not oversalt the soup.

If you and your company like cilantro, garnish each bowl with a small sprig.

Oriental Stock

This stock can be used for Oriental soups and vegetable sautés. We use it in Tofu-Miso Stew (page 150). One or another kind of dried mushroom are often available in larger supermarkets. They are also available at Japanese, Chinese, and Italian food shops. Kombu is a kind of dried seaweed available at Japanese markets and some natural food stores.

2 carrots, peeled
1 celery rib
1 chard leaf and stem, or several
   lettuce leaves
3 scallions
3–4 dry shiitake or Chinese
   black mushrooms or ½ ounce
   other dried mushroom
6-inch piece kombu, if available

2-inch piece gobo (burdock), if
   available
small handful lentil sprouts or
   large handful mung bean or
   soybean sprouts
4½ cups water
1 teaspoon dark sesame oil
1 tablespoon tamari
salt

Makes 3 cups

Scrub the vegetables and cut into large pieces.

Put all the ingredients except the salt into a pot, bring to a boil, and simmer 25 minutes. (All right, what if you can't get any dried mushrooms? Omit them and keep on cooking. Use fresh mushrooms, which provide some flavor, even though they don't have the intensity of the dried ones.)

Remove the mushrooms and set them aside for another use. Then strain the stock and boil until it is reduced to 3 cups.

Taste for salt and add if necessary.

Variation for non-Oriental dishes: Omit gobo, sesame oil, and tamari. (Mushrooms, kombu, and sprouts can also be omitted if not available.)

Add a small onion, a bay leaf, 2 cloves garlic, pinch of thyme, and a bit of black pepper.

Mushroom Stock

This flavorful stock can be used advantageously in any number of soups and sauces. The more mushrooms, the stronger the mushroom flavor will be. Dried mushrooms will contribute a rich, woodsy flavor. Mushroom stock freezes well, so make up a larger quantity and freeze some of it.

2 tablespoons oil
4–8 ounces fresh mushrooms,
  roughly chopped
1 onion, sliced
1 medium potato, washed but
  not peeled, roughly chopped
1 carrot, peeled and sliced
4–5 cloves garlic, coarsely
  chopped
1 bay leaf

½ teaspoon dried thyme
pinch dried savory
1 tablespoon nutritional yeast
3 quarts water
2 tablespoons tamari soy sauce
10 peppercorns
½ ounce dried mushrooms,
  shiitake, or Italian (optional)
salt to taste

Yields 2 quarts

Heat the oil in a soup pot and add the mushrooms, onions, potatoes, carrots, garlic, and aromatics.

Cook over medium-high heat for 10 minutes, stirring frequently. Add the yeast and cook another 5 minutes. Then add the water, tamari, peppercorns, and dried mushrooms.

Bring to a boil, then reduce the heat and simmer 45 minutes, by which time the liquid should be reduced by a third.

At the end of the cooking time, taste and adjust with salt. (Note: Salt becomes more concentrated as the liquid reduces.)

Pour the stock through a strainer lined with cheesecloth, pressing down gently on the vegetables to extract their juices. Discard the vegetables.

Refrigerate or freeze the stock until needed.

Salads &
Salad Dressings

BROWSING IN THE GARDEN

Just picked
leaf of lettuce, not cold
and crisp, but throbbing warm
with bitter earth juice,
a wrinkled green and purple
landscape gleaming in sunlight.

In darkness this velvet
flesh meets my teeth
and tongue and cheek,
ever so intimately:
soft persistent crunches
render lettuce speechless.
Our juices mingle,
flow as one the unseen
pathways appearing as mountains
or someone just about to wash a plate.

Salads & Salad Dressings

Here we have, if I may be so bold to say, one of the great joys of life—a great joy because salads can offer us what is fully ripe and freshly flavorful, the pick of the fields brought to the table in its prime.

Especially in the heat of summer, salads are an essential element of all our lunches and dinners. This section includes a variety of salads, all of which we serve in addition to a more standard repertoire of garden greens, either unembellished or combined with some combination of tomatoes, avocados, olives, grated cheese, and croutons.

There are two green salads, two Chinese cabbage salads (a cabbage especially suitable for salads because it is more tender and juicy than the usual varieties), two main course salads, and three slightly unusual salads, the avocados with grilled red pepper sauce being especially appealing. Two simple relishes and a few dressings round out the section.

I must confess the best recipe for salad is not included. The best I know is to walk through gardens a few steps from home, forget the recipes, and follow your nose.

Mixed Green Salad with Grapefruit, Avocado & Lime-Cumin Vinaigrette

Inspired by a North African recipe, this very pretty and refreshing salad is a marvelous complement to rich dishes. Everything may be prepared hours in advance, with only the slicing of the avocados and tossing of the salad left for the end.

For the salad:
5 large handfuls mixed greens: Romaine, spinach, oakleaf, butter, or red lettuces
2 ruby grapefruit
1–2 avocados

For the vinaigrette:
grated peel of 4 limes
3 tablespoons lime juice
1 teaspoon salt
½ teaspoon each cumin & coriander seeds, ground in spice mill
½ teaspoon paprika
½ teaspoon dry mustard

pinch of chili powder
1 clove garlic, finely minced or pounded to a paste
⅓ to ½ cup olive oil
1–2 tablespoons coarsely chopped cilantro
2 scallions minced, both green and white parts

Serves 4

Wash the greens, dry them well, then tear into bite-sized pieces.

Section the grapefruit, removing seeds and membranes.

To make the vinaigrette, combine the lime peel, juice, salt, spices, and garlic, and stir to dissolve the salt.

Add olive oil to taste (dip in a lettuce leaf and try it), minced scallions, and chopped cilantro.

Whisk lightly to combine.

Shortly before serving, slice the avocados.

Now you have a choice of assembly:

ONE: Put the dressing with the avocado and grapefruit in the bottom of a large salad bowl, add the mixed greens and toss, or,

TWO: Douse the avocado and grapefruit with dressing and then pour off the excess dressing. Then toss the mixed greens with enough dressing to moisten the leaves but not to leave them dripping. Finally, garnish the dressed greens with the dressed grapefruit and avocado.

Spinach Salad with Feta Cheese, Red Onions & Olives

A tangy, dramatic-looking variation on a Greek salad, this dish is nice with the yogurt soup (page 64) or the moussaka (page 170). Bold flavors.

For the salad:
1 bunch fresh spinach leaves
2–3 ounces feta cheese
¼ cup (or more) pickled red onions (page 86)
6 Kalamata olives, OR 12 or more Nicoise olives
½ teaspoon fresh mint, minced

For the vinaigrette:
2 ½-inch-wide strips of lemon peel
1–2 tablespoons lemon juice
freshly grated black pepper
clove of garlic, pressed or finely minced
6 tablespoons fruity olive oil

Serves 4-6

Cut the stems off the spinach and immerse the leaves in at least two changes of cold water to remove all traces of sand and fine soil.

Dry well, then cut into pieces and place the spinach in a salad bowl.

Crumble the feta cheese on top.

Cut the onions into 1½-inch pieces or as desired. Scatter them over the cheese.

Remove the pits from the olives by pressing them under the palms of your hand, then pulling out the loosened pits. Chop coarsely, then sprinkle the olives along with the mint on top of the salad.

To make the vinaigrette, slice the strips of lemon peel into very fine slivers and combine with the lemon juice, pepper, and garlic in a small bowl.

Whisk in the olive oil. Taste with a leaf of spinach and adjust for tartness if necessary. Do not add salt, as the feta cheese and olives are salty.

Pour the vinaigrette over the salad, and toss well.

Spiced Rice Salad

This rice has been dressed up with many tasty tidbits swirled into it: slivers, slices, dots, and dices of color and texture, all on a background of white. A spicy dressing accents everything. Be sure to cut the pieces of onion and pepper small enough so that their texture and flavor do not intrude and take over. Take some time to cut things carefully and beautifully, and your salad will be a distinctive and elegant treat.

For the salad:
½ cup golden raisins
½ cup dried apricots
½ cup almonds OR pine nuts
1 stalk celery, thinly sliced
1 medium red onion, finely diced
1 red bell pepper, finely diced or sliced, OR ½ red and ½ green bell pepper, finely diced or sliced
juice and zest of 2 lemons
2 cups white rice, pearl or short-grain
1 avocado, cut in ½-inch chunks

For the dressing:
2 cloves garlic
½ teaspoon salt
½ teaspoon cumin seed (whole or ground)
2 tablespoons sherry wine vinegar
6–7 tablespoons light olive oil
black pepper, freshly grated
½ bunch cilantro, some set aside for garnish, the rest minced

Makes 6–7 cups
Preheat oven to 325°

Put the apricots and raisins in separate bowls and cover them with boiling water. Let them soak for 30 minutes and then drain. Slice the apricots crosswise into slivers or strips.

Toast the nuts in a preheated 325° oven, stirring occasionally, until golden (about 10 minutes for the almonds or 5 minutes for the pine nuts). If using almonds, chop them coarsely. Set aside.

Combine the celery, onions, and peppers with the juice and zest of the lemons. When the dried fruit is ready, add it. Set this aside to let the flavors become acquainted while the rice is cooked and the dressing made.

Prepare the dressing so that it will be ready when the rice is cooked. Pound the garlic with the salt and the cumin seed (whole or ground) in a mortar (or press the garlic and mix it with the salt and cumin). Mix well with the vinegar, and then slowly whisk in the oil to make a vinaigrette. Salt and adjust tartness to taste (adding a little oil or vinegar). Add the black pepper and minced cilantro.

To cook the rice, boil it for about 15 minutes in 2 quarts of lightly salted water, like pasta. When it is cooked, but still firm rather than mushy, drain the rice in a fine sieve or colander lined with cheesecloth (or a clean dish towel). Rinse it briefly in warm water, shake off as much excess water as possible, and while still warm, toss with the dressing.

Let the rice sit with the dressing for 5–10 minutes and then mix in the vegetables and dried fruits. Shortly before serving, add the avocado, the nuts, and the coarsely chopped cilantro. (Coriander seed can be used to good effect in place of the fresh cilantro. Pound ½ teaspoon with the garlic when making the dressing.)

Taste for salt and pepper or any other added effects you may dream up at this last minute. Serve on lettuce leaves (butter or red leaf perhaps?). If the occasion permits, the lettuce leaves can be wrapped around the rice and eaten with your fingers.

White Bean Salad

White beans never had it so good. This hearty, multicolored salad can be a main course salad or a first-rate picnic food. Especially aromatic when warm and freshly dressed, the salad may be served immediately, or allowed to cool before serving, particularly in hot weather. Do not let the long list of ingredients intimidate you, as it is not essential to include every last thing, and you may have other ideas of what you'd like to include: zucchini, peas, potatoes—look and see what you have around.

For the salad:
1½ cups navy beans, cleaned and sorted
several sage leaves
a bay leaf
3 cloves of garlic
2 green peppers, diced small or slivered
2–3 scallions, green and white parts both, minced or thin sliced
¼ cup parsley, minced
2 tablespoons chervil
2 tablespoons chives, sliced into thin rings
1 teaspoon each fresh thyme and marjoram, minced
¼ cup pickled red onion, diced or minced (page 86)
6–8 Greek olives, pitted and minced
2 large ripe tomatoes, cored, seeded, and diced, OR 3–4 sun-dried
    tomatoes, diced or slivered
peel of one lemon, finely diced
salt & black pepper

Serves 4–6

Soak the beans overnight and then simmer them in 2 quarts water with the sage, bay leaf, and garlic until tender and soft, about 2 hours (or pressure cook for 15 minutes).

While the beans are cooking, prepare the remaining ingredients and make the vinaigrette. If you are not too preoccupied with more important matters, let the colors, flavors, and aromas come home to your heart, and let your heart resume its original freshness and creativity.

For the vinaigrette:
2–3 cloves garlic
½ teapoon salt
1½–2 tablespoons Dijon mustard
3 tablespoons strong red wine or sherry wine vinegar
⅔ cup olive oil

Pound the garlic and salt into a paste, and combine with the mustard and vinegar. Whisk in the olive oil. Taste for seasoning, but do not be alarmed by the strength of the dressing—the beans can take it.

Once the beans are soft, drain them in a colander. While they are still hot, gently toss them with the vinaigrette and the other ingredients. Taste and season as desired with salt, pepper, additional herbs, mustard, or what have you.

Chinese Cabbage Salad with Orange & Tahini Dressing

Chinese cabbage is tender and mild-flavored with a slight peppery quality, and carries dressings well. Available at Chinese and Japanese markets, Chinese cabbage can also often be found in supermarkets now.

For the salad:
1 small or ½ large Chinese cabbage
4–5 oranges

Serves 4–6

Slice the cabbage into quarters and then into thin strips crosswise or at an angle crosswise.

To get the full orange color, cut the peel off the oranges. Cut the oranges in chunks or rounds.

Set aside a few rounds for garnish and mix the rest of the oranges in with the cabbage.

For the dressing:
½ tablespoon lemon or lime juice
1 tablespoon soy sauce
1 tablespoon apple cider vinegar
pinch of salt
1½ tablespoons water
pepper
clove of garlic, pressed
1½ tablespoons dark sesame oil
¼ cup sesame butter or tahini

Mix together the first seven ingredients and set aside.

Blend together the sesame butter and oil, then whisk into the other mixture. The dressing should be thick; once it is on the cabbage, it will thin out.

Toss the dressing together with the cabbage and oranges and garnish with the orange slices.

Chinese Cabbage Salad with Garlic Vinaigrette

Aside from the Chinese cabbage, all the other ingredients in this salad are from the West. Again, the cabbage blends in well with the other ingredients.

For the salad:
1 small or ½ large Chinese cabbage
1–1½ cups Gruyere cheese, grated, OR *Monterey Jack, Gouda, or Edam*
½–¾ cup black olives, sliced

For the dressing:
2 tablespoons vinegar
¼ teaspoon salt
2–3 cloves garlic, pressed
⅝ cup olive oil

Serves 4–6

Slice the cabbage into quarters and then into thin strips crosswise or at an angle crosswise.

Mix the cabbage with the grated cheese and sliced olives.

For the dressing, mix the vinegar together with the salt and garlic, then gradually whisk in the olive oil.

Toss the salad with the dressing. Depending on the amount of cabbage you use, you may not need all the dressing.

Taste for salt.

Carrot Ginger Salad with Golden Raisins & Sour Cream

Use carrots with a sweet, full flavor that are not too woody. These two roots, carrot and ginger, go well together, and their natural sweetness is enhanced by the raisins.

1 cup golden raisins
1–2 teaspoons peeled, fresh ginger, finely grated
½ cup sour cream
grated rind of 1 lemon
1 teaspoon lemon juice
salt
4 cups carrots, peeled and grated

Serves 4–6

Cover the raisins with hot water, let stand for 20 minutes to plump them up, then drain.

Mix the ginger together with the sour cream, lemon rind and lemon juice, then salt to taste.

Combine the carrots, raisins, and dressing. Toss well.

Adjust seasoning. The raisins should make it sweet enough, but if not, add a little honey or sugar.

Variations: Orange juice and rind can also be used. If using yogurt in place of sour cream, you may want to add a little honey.

If you like, garnish the salad with some finely-sliced scallions.

Avocado Salad with Grilled Red Pepper Sauce

Bright and pretty, this salad has the sweet, smokey flavor of grilled red peppers.

1 large red bell pepper
1 medium clove garlic
1 tablespoon fruity olive oil
1 teaspoon sherry vinegar
salt & freshly ground pepper
2 avocados at room temperature
Nicoise or other small black olives to garnish

Serves 4

Char the bell pepper whole over a burner, turning it on a fork until thoroughly blackened on all sides.

Put the pepper in a covered dish or closed jar for several minutes to steam. Then peel off the skin (water—either in a bowl or running—makes the peeling easier). Remove seeds and ribs.

Rinse the pepper, then pat dry.

Roughly chop the pepper and the garlic, then pound both vigorously in a mortar until you have a coarsely textured sauce. (A good pinch of coarse sea salt will speed this process.) You may prefer to use a blender or food processor.

Whisk in the olive oil and vinegar, then season with salt and pepper to taste.

Slice the avocados and arrange on individual serving plates.

Spoon the sauce over the slices and garnish with olives.

Pineapple Jicama Salad with Avocado, Chilies & Lime

This is a zesty and refreshing salad in hot weather. It can be either really mouth-awakening and eye-watering or mildly pleasing, depending on the availability of ingredients and your taste for chilies. Pineapple you know; jicama you may not know—it is a delightfully crunchy vegetable from Mexico.

For the salad:
3 large leaves Romaine lettuce, sliced into strips, or whole small leaves
1/2 red bell pepper, cut into thin strips
1/4 cup pickled red onion (page 86), OR 1/4 red onion, cut crosswise into thin arcs
cilantro leaves
1 small pineapple (about 2 cups), cut into bite-sized pieces
1 cup jicama, cut into thin matchsticks, OR 1 apple, sliced
1 poblano chili, cut into thin rings, OR 1 green bell pepper
12 sweet-smelling cherry tomatoes
finely diced fresh hot chili (optional)
1–2 avocados, cut into chunks

For the dressing:
juice and grated peel of 2 limes
2 teaspoons sherry vinegar or balsamic vinegar
2–4 tablespoons chopped cilantro
1/2 teaspoon salt
1/4 cup olive oil
1/4–1/2 cup sour cream

Serves 4

Set aside the lettuce and also some of the pepper strips, onions, and cilantro leaves for garnish.

Combine the remaining salad ingredients, except for the avocado, in a large bowl.

To make the dressing, whisk together the lime juice, peel, vinegar, cilantro, and salt.

Whisk in the olive oil and then the sour cream. Adjust taste for tartness and salt.

Add the dressing to the salad and toss gently with a large rubber spatula or your hands. Then fold in the avocado chunks.

Mound the salad on a platter, rim the sides with the lettuce, and garnish with the reserved vegetables and cilantro.

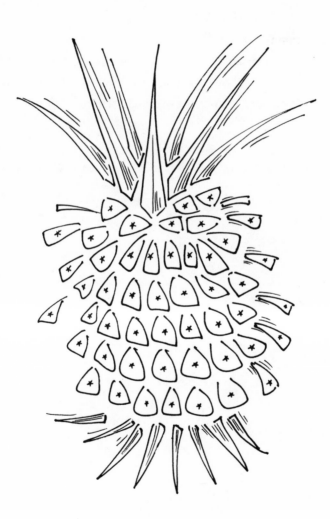

Pickled Red Onions

A simple and straightforward recipe for making onions ready for salad.

red onions
boiling water
apple cider vinegar

Slice the red onions thinly.

Put them in a colander and pour boiling water over them.

Remove the onions to a bowl and add enough vinegar to cover them.

Let them marinate several hours or overnight. Drain off excess vinegar before serving.

Store in the refrigerator.

Herbs like oregano, thyme, rosemary may be added as well. Follow your nose.

Mama Sawyer's Cucumber Relish

Michael and Ken grew up on this, so when they got to Tassajara, they passed it on to the guest cooks. We have made it to everyone's gustatory delight, and found it especially good on cheese sandwiches, melted and unmelted. This recipe makes a bunch, but it keeps, refrigerated.

9 large cucumbers, chopped medium fine
4 large onions, chopped medium fine
salt
3 cups vinegar
3 cups sugar
½ cup flour
1 tablespoon celery seed
1 tablespoon mustard seed
½ teaspoon turmeric

Sprinkle the cucumbers and onions with salt and leave overnight. Drain off any excess liquid.

Combine the remaining ingredients in a saucepan with the drained vegetables. Bring to a boil and cook for five minutes.

Our Salad Dressing & Variations

Salad dressings are one of those mysterious and alchemical mixtures which can be heavenly and tantalizing, or abysmal. They are not only a matter of taste, but a matter of lifestyle. In dressing preparation, many rituals are ascribed to: for example, rubbing the bowl with garlic; tossing with oil, then with vinegar; or everything in the blender and "zap!" The simpler the dressing—and this recipe is quite simple—the more it depends on the quality of the ingredients: a subtle and refined sherry wine vinegar; a fragrant, fruity olive oil.

One's salad dressing matures with one's experience. Dressing can develop, change, or remain the single constant in a life of change. Complex, crafted, laid back, or thrown together—if you want to know about people, check out their salad dressing and how they make it. But for now, check out our dressing and how we make it.

clove of garlic, small
¾ to 1 teaspoon salt
2 tablespoons sherry wine vinegar
¾ cup olive oil, good and fruity (if it smells like castor oil, it's rancid)
freshly grated black pepper

Crush the garlic in a press or mash it in a mortar and pestle. Let the garlic, salt, and vinegar sit together in a bowl for at least 15 minutes to get acquainted.

Slowly whisk in the olive oil. Make sure it is well mixed.

Dress the salad so that it is moistened, but not dripping. Have the pepper mill handy for those who like it.

Variations:

For an herb vinaigrette: Add chopped fresh herbs right before serving. (Then they will look fresh, instead of turning grey and slimey.)

For a mustard vinaigrette: Add ½ tablespoon or more of prepared mustard to the basic recipe.

For a lemon or lime vinaigrette: Use lemon or lime juice as part or all of the vinegar.

For a sour cream vinaigrette: Use sour cream as part of the oil.

88

For a garlic vinaigrette: Add an additional clove or two of garlic.

For a garlic-mustard vinaigrette: Add an additional clove of garlic to the mustard vinaigrette. This strongly flavored dressing is especially appetizing on cold vegetable salads (e.g. blanched carrots, peas, yellow squash, or with cherry tomatoes).

To make this cold vegetable salad, first blanch the vegetables, and then mix the dressing with the vegetables while they are still hot and slightly crunchy. Cover the bowl with a lid and allow to cool. It may be necessary to drain the vegetables before serving.

Or skip the recipes and do it your way, incorporating the ritual you know.

Avocado Yogurt Dressing

Try this dressing with sliced cukes, tomato slices, and thin strips of green bell pepper.

One large, ripe avocado
1 cup yogurt
pinch of salt
1 tablespoon lemon juice
1 large clove garlic

Blend ingredients together until smooth, taste for seasoning.

Tahini Tamari Dressing

Good as a dressing, this also makes a tasty dip for raw vegetables.

½ cup tahini (sesame butter)
½ cup orange juice
3 cloves garlic, pressed
soy sauce to taste

Blend ingredients together until smooth.

Adjust seasoning.

May be thinned with water, orange juice, or oil.

Sauces & Spreads

NO MEASURING UP

Now I make time
to peel potatoes, wash lettuce,
and boil beets, to scrub floors,
clean sinks, and empty trash.
Absorbed in the everyday,
I find time to unbind, unwind,
to invite whole body, mind,
breath, thought, and wild impulse
to join, to wallow in the task.

No time lost thinking
that somewhere else is better.
No time lost imagining
getting more elsewhere.
No way to tell this moment
does not measure up.

Hand me the spatula:
now is the time to taste what is.

Sauces & Spreads

The sauces here are all pretty basic and straightforward. Some we use quite regularly for particular dishes: e.g., the Nut Loaf Sauce for Cheese and Nut Loaf, the Tartar Sauce for Tofu Cutlets. Others we use more widely: the Vegetable Bechamels and Spinach or Sorrel Sauce turn up on vegetables, grains, omelettes, timbale.

The spreads we use primarily to help make sandwiches more interesting.

You take it from here, okay?

Nut Loaf Sauce

We often serve this with the Cheese and Nut Loaf (page 162), but its sweet nuttiness, somewhat reminiscent of meat gravies, also goes well with green leafy vegetables such as chard, kale, mustard, and spinach. If you are unfamiliar with nutritional yeast, begin with the smaller amount. "Good Tasting" nutritional yeast is the brand whose flavor we like the best.

2–2½ cups mushroom stock, vegetable stock, or water
2–4 tablespoons nutritional yeast
¼ cup unbleached white flour
5 tablespoons light sesame or light olive oil
1 tablespoon butter
2 tablespoons soy sauce
2 teaspoons Dijon mustard
freshly grated pepper
1 large clove of garlic, pounded to a paste or put through a press
¼ cup sherry

Makes 2½–3 cups

Put the stock on to heat, so that it is boiling when needed.

Toast the yeast and flour in a heavy saucepan, stirring over medium-low heat until fragrant and lightly browned.

Add the oil and butter and cook for 5 minutes.

Slowly whisk in 2 cups of the boiling stock, then lower the heat and simmer gently for 20 minutes.

Add the soy sauce, mustard, pepper, garlic, and sherry. Cook for another 5 minutes. If necessary, thin with additional stock.

Taste for salt. Adjust other seasonings as desired.

Tartar Sauce with Fresh Basil

We use this primarily with our breaded tofu dish, but also sometimes as a sandwich spread. The exact proportions on this are not so precise; it is largely a matter of taste how much of each ingredient you use.

1 cup mayonnaise
1 tablespoon Dijon mustard
2 tablespoons red onion, minced
2 tablespoons pickles, minced (choice of sweet or dill)
2 tablespoons green olives, minced
2 tablespoons capers, chopped (optional)
¼ cup fresh basil, finely sliced and chopped
wine vinegar or lemon juice

Makes 2 cups

Start by mixing together the mayonnaise and mustard. Add the minced and chopped ingredients, using less of any one you have your doubts about. Omit the ones you do not have.

Add wine vinegar or lemon juice to taste—probably a few teaspoons full.

Mustard Sauce

Inspired by a book on medieval cookery, this sauce can be used as a dip or as a dressing for vegetables or potato salad.

Dijon mustard
brown sugar or honey
light olive oil (optional)

Sweeten the mustard to taste with brown sugar or honey.

Add a little olive oil to soften the flavor. Try it with a piece of vegetable.

Serve chilled with an arranged platter of cold vegetables such as blanched carrots, broccoli, cauliflower, new potatoes, zucchini, fresh tomatoes, cucumbers, and peppers.

Vegetable Bechamel

The bechamel sauce—made from butter, flour, and milk—may be lightly seasoned by cooking vegetables in the milk, before it is added to the butter-flour roux. In fact, almost any dish using a bechamel can be improved by using vegetables in the milk. (The idea came to us from Richard Olney.) Listed are a number of vegetables you may want to use. Vegetable-flavored bechamels work well with vegetables and grains, in baked dishes, or as a simple sauce.

Vegetables, a choice:
1 medium or 2 small zucchini, medium diced
mushrooms, large handful, wiped clean and coarsely chopped
3 or 4 large cloves garlic, peeled
dried mushrooms, ½ ounce
1 medium leek, washed, coarsely chopped
1 or 2 stalks of celery, medium diced
1 or 2 bay leaves
1 medium yellow onion, coarsely chopped
4 cups milk
3 tablespoons butter
4 tablespoons flour
salt

Makes 4 cups

Pick out and prepare the vegetable(s) you want, and simmer them in the milk for 20–30 minutes. Milk tends to burn when it is boiled, so be quite careful not to overheat it.

Melt the butter in a saucepan (over low flame), stir in the flour, and cook for several minutes, until you can no longer taste the raw flavor of the flour.

Strain the milk through a sieve to remove the vegetables.

Add the milk slowly to the cooked butter-flour roux, stirring vigorously, using a flat-bottomed utensil to scrape the bottom. Keep adding the milk as the mixture thickens, until all the milk is added.

Salt to taste.

If necessary, heat to serving temperature, stirring often.

If not using right away, keep the sauce warm in a double boiler. Or, cool and reheat later, being careful not to scorch it by using too high a flame.

Spinach or Sorrel Sauce

These "green bechamels" prove excellent on vegetable timbales. They also work well as a sauce for baked eggs or omelettes (e.g. mushroom-onion omelette with sorrel sauce).

4 cups bechamel sauce
1 large bunch spinach or sorrel
salt

Make up a bechamel sauce as above omitting the vegetables in the milk.

Put the greens into a heavy sauce pan with about ½ inch of lightly salted water.

Cook at a high temperature, stirring frequently, until the greens are "melted." Drain the greens, and reserve the liquid for soup or stock.

Push the greens through a sieve or liquefy in a blender. Then whisk the green purée into the bechamel.

Salt to taste.

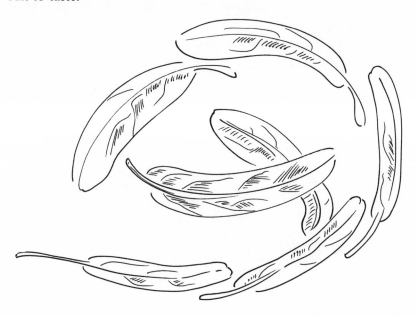

Herbed Cream Cheese

This is just to say that herbed cream cheese is delicious—and versatile: for cheese sandwiches, for chip and vegetable dip, and, if piped from a pastry bag, for quite decorative hors d'oeuvres on small squares of bread. Also, the recipe is simple.

2 cups cream cheese
½ cup milk or light cream
2 tablespoons fresh herbs (finely chopped)

For smoothness and easy spreading, mix the cream cheese with warmed milk or cream.

Mix in the fresh herbs (thyme, chives, rosemary, marjoram, dill, tarragon, basil—from your herb garden, of course). Use more or less to taste.

Put into serving bowl or pipe with a pastry bag.

Garnish with separated chive blossoms, marjoram leaves or flowers.

Variations: Add up to ½ cup of goat cheese, ricotta, or feta in place of the cream cheese.

Add garlic, olives, or sun-dried tomatoes.

Yogurt Cheese

This fresh, slightly tart cheese provides a cool and light accompaniment to crackers and breads, especially pita, buckwheat, or rye. Amenable to a variety of seasonings, yogurt cheese is easily made by draining the water out of the yogurt. The longer it's drained, the harder the cheese gets.

1 quart yogurt, plain
salt
herbs (see below)

One quart of yogurt yields 1½ cups of cheese

Line a sieve with a large double-layer square of cheesecloth that has been dampened in cool water. Pour the yogurt into the sieve and tie the corners of the cheesecloth together to make a bag.

Suspend the bag from a spoon over a deep bowl or pot to drain.

Do your laundry or take in a flick. Check back in about 3 hours to see if the yogurt has reached the consistency you desire. If not, let the draining continue, checking periodically, until it has. (I've also tried this with a coffee filter, but it takes longer to drain.)

Remove the yogurt from the cloth and season to taste with a little salt.

If fresh herbs are intended, add them at least an hour before serving so the flavors have a chance to develop. Generous amounts can be used.

Herb possibilities:
fresh dill	*caraway*
cilantro and green onions	*basil*
chili powder	*thyme, marjoram, and parsley*
sun-dried tomatoes	*lovage*
olives	*flat-leaf parsley and chives*
garlic	

Almond Paté

This savory, flavorful nut paste claims the distinction of being possibly the most requested recipe during guest season. We use it as a sandwich spread and it's great to serve with fresh celery or fennel, or as a spread with crackers. Try this paté as a filling for mushrooms or as a "nut chutney" for grains or vegetables.

1 cup minced onion
1 tablespoon butter
½ teaspoon freshly ground
   cumin
½ teaspoon savory
½ teaspoon fine herbs
1 cup raw almonds, ground
   fairly fine
½ cup plus 2 tablespoons bread
   crumbs, toasted in the oven

2 tablespoons freshly minced
   parsley
1 teaspoon tamari
1 small clove garlic, minced
salt & freshly ground pepper
2–4 tablespoons mayonnaise or
   sour cream
lemon slices

Yields 1 cup

Cook the onions in the butter over low heat with the cumin, savory, and fine herbs until they are soft.

Scrape the onion mixture into a bowl. Using your fingers, work in the almonds, bread crumbs, parsley, tamari, and garlic.

Taste and season with salt and pepper.

Gradually mix in the mayonnaise or sour cream until the mixture holds together.

Shape it into a log or press it into a serving dish and garnish with overlapping slices of lemon.

A Few Grain, Bean
& Side Dishes

AN ORDINARY DAY

To realize true nature, we
study the body and mind of Reality.
Will you have this body and mind?
these grains and beans?
Will you settle for this body and mind?
these vegetables and fruits?
This body!
This mind!
The body and mind of Reality
are not different than this
body and mind right now,
but to know it fully,
we must examine and investigate,
actualize it through and through.

What we really want
waits within
the ordinary.

A Few Grain, Bean & Side Dishes

With dinner we often serve a grain dish and a vegetable dish in addition to an entree and a salad, but having put so many "fundamental" recipes into *Tassajara Cooking* (1973), I have included only a few here.

Aside from the recipes—pilaf, garbanzo stew, baked tomatoes, and baked onions (the latter two frequently and regularly)—we actually prepare for guests, this section also includes some longterm student favorites: brown rice, sesame soybeans, and tofu cabbage grill.

Plus, I give you two of my own lighthearted summer inventions, for peas and spinach. Check them out and don't laugh, until you have tried them.

Properly Cooked Brown Rice

All right, all you brown rice fans out there, here is a method that always produces perfectly cooked rice. It works for both short grain and long grain brown rice. You need a pot with a tight-fitting lid and plenty of time to contemplate.

Note: The tight-fitting lid is most important. If a lid is dented or the wrong size, the steam will escape and the rice will need more liquid or more time; how much more of either is hard to determine. If your lid does not fit well, cover the pot with foil, put the lid in place, and set a weight on top to keep it as tight as possible.

1 cup brown rice
2 cups water
½ teaspoon salt
1 tablespoon butter or oil

Yields 2 cups cooked rice

Rinse and drain the rice, then soak it in the water for 1 hour.

Put both rice and water into a heavy saucepan.

Add the salt and butter and bring to a boil.

Immediately reduce the heat to its lowest setting and cover the pot with a tight-fitting lid. Cook the rice for 1 hour undisturbed.

Watch TV, prepare other dishes for dinner, or do your yoga asanas, but *don't look in the pot*. The rice needs seclusion to turn out properly.

To tell when it's done just listen to the pot: no more bubbling, but a subtle, yet distinct crackling or popping sound. The rice on the bottom is becoming toasted.

Leave the pot tightly covered. Just before serving, gently fluff the grains with a fork.

If properly cooked and properly eaten (100 chews per mouthful), the brown rice will properly become you.

Bulgur Pilaf with Vegetables

Enjoy the grainy toastiness of wheat with flecks of colorful vegetables and mushrooms. The mushroom stock intensifies the flavor in this recipe adopted from Madhur Jaffrey.

For the mushroom stock:
3 cups water
small handful of dried mushrooms (½ ounce) or ½ cup fresh
  mushrooms
2 cloves garlic
cleaned stalks of mushrooms (caps used in pilaf)
½ onion, sliced

Combine ingredients and bring to a boil, reduce to simmering for ½ hour.
Strain before using.

For the pilaf:
4 tablespoons vegetable oil
1 cup red onions, small diced
1 teaspoon salt
1 cup thinly sliced mushroom caps
½ cup carrots, small diced or ½ cup pimiento, well-drained and small
  diced
2 cups bulgur wheat
2½ cups mushroom stock

Serves 4–6

Heat the oil in a heavy 2 quart pot with a lid.

Add the onions and the salt. Sauté until the onions are just beginning to get tender.

Add the mushrooms and other veggies and sauté for another minute or two.

Add the bulgur. Stir and sauté until the grains are well coated with oil.

Add the 2½ cups of stock and bring to a boil.

Cover, reduce the heat, and simmer for 25 minutes.
Turn off the heat. Put a dish towel between the lid and the pot.
Allow to set for 20 minutes.
Serve hot.

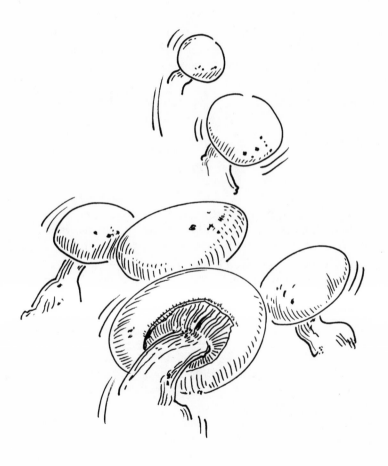

Garbanzo Stew

Garbanzo beans have a tendency to be dry and uninteresting, but in this recipe they are surrounded with spicy juiciness. Stews take a while to stew, but the process is quite simple, and the results—in this case, a dish of surprising taste and beautiful colors—are worth waiting for.

1 cup dried garbanzo beans (chickpeas)
1 medium yellow onion, diced
3 cloves garlic, pressed
1 tablespoon nutritional yeast
½ teaspoon cumin
1 medium-large red potato, cubed
1 small turnip, cubed
curry spices
paprika

dried sage
1 stalk celery, sliced
½ green pepper, cut into squares
1 cup mushrooms, whole or halved
red wine
1½ cups canned tomatoes, drained, chopped
basil
marjoram
salt & pepper

Makes 1½ quarts

Soak the beans overnight. Pressure cook them for 30 minutes. Sauté the onions for several minutes and then add the garlic, nutritional yeast, and cumin. Continue cooking until the onions are translucent.

In a saucepan, combine the cooked beans and their cooking liquid with the sautéed onions, the potato cubes, and the turnip cubes. Then season to taste with the curry spices, paprika, sage, and salt. Simmer until cooked, about 40 minutes.

Meanwhile, stir-fry the celery, peppers, and mushrooms for a few minutes. Then add the red wine and tomatoes, and simmer a few minutes until tender-crisp. Set aside until the stew is nearly cooked, and then add this mixture to the stew. Season with the basil, marjoram, salt, and pepper. Make sure everything is hot before serving.

Sesame Soybeans

Some more down-home cooking, this is a recipe that we prepare for ourselves in the winter. Though not a guest season recipe, sesame soybeans are much requested. Students say, "You're going to put in sesame soybeans, aren't you?" So, for all of you mountain yogis and aspiring mountain yogis, here it is.

1½ cups soybeans
water
¾ cup sesame butter (tahini)
soy sauce
salt & pepper

Serves 4

Soak the beans in water overnight.

Drain off—but reserve—the water. Measure three cups of water, including the soaking water, in which to cook the beans.

Simmer the beans for 3 hours or pressure cook them at 15 pounds pressure for 30 minutes. Make sure the beans are quite soft.

Drain off the cooking liquid and reserve it.

Thin the tahini with some of the cooking liquid, and add this to the beans. Add more liquid to bring the beans to the desired consistency.

Season with soy sauce, salt, and pepper.

Tofu Cabbage Grill

This side dish is one of our favorites. We even eat it for breakfast in the winter.

1 block of tofu
small head of cabbage (green, red, or Chinese)
2 large or 3 smaller cloves of garlic
fresh ginger, a thumb-sized chunk
1 tablespoon sesame oil
soy oil, for frying
soy sauce

Serves 4–6

Press and drain the tofu, then cut it into chunks. Cut the cabbage into shreds. Press the garlic, grate the ginger, and mix these two with the sesame oil.

Fry the tofu in soy oil (or other light oil) on a fairly high heat to brown it. Add the ginger-garlic paste and continue frying another minute or so. Remove from the pan.

Re-oil the pan and cook the cabbage over moderate heat until done. Add the tofu.

Season with soy sauce, adding more ginger or garlic to taste.

Serve when everything is hot.

"Chinese" Cauliflower

This cauliflower is about as "Chinese" as chop suey. We've never made it for the guests, but I liked it so much I asked Iva for the recipe.

cauliflower
butter
salt
Szechwan pepper
white pepper
fresh herbs: thyme, rosemary, chives, parsley

Sauté the cauliflower in the butter in a large skillet over moderately high heat for a few minutes.

Add the salt, the Szechwan pepper, and seasonings. Put on a lid, reduce the heat, and let it steam until done.

Baked Onions with Balsamic Vinegar

Balsamic vinegar is a full-flavored, dark, intense, well-aged vinegar, available at specialty food shops. In this recipe, it provides the finishing touch to onions sweet, soft, and mellow from a lengthy baking. We often serve this as a side dish to pasta. The recipe is about as simple as can be, but it takes a while, so, if possible, bake the onions a day ahead.

red onions, large but not gigantic
Balsamic vinegar

Preheat oven to 400°

Line the bottom of a baking sheet with foil to catch the drippings (or put a rack in a baking pan with water underneath as you would meat). Bake the whole unpeeled onions at 400° for 1½ hours or until they are completely soft and limp.

Let cool enough to peel, cut off the ends, and remove the skin. Prepare to give those onions their Balsamic bath.

Cut the onions in half, nestle them into a high-sided casserole or baking pan, and cover with Balsamic vinegar. (After use, the vinegar can be kept and reused once it has been strained through a double layer of cheesecloth or a coffee filter.)

Let the onions marinate for at least an hour before serving.

Baked Tomatoes with Herbs

This simple and straightforward recipe is as good as the tomatoes. The bright red, plump tomatoes bring a bounteous feeling to the meal.

4 good-sized, flavorful tomatoes
olive oil
marjoram, dried
basil, dried
2 cloves garlic, minced (optional)
salt & pepper
1 tablespoon fresh basil, minced or strips

Serves 4
Preheat oven to 350°

Remove the stem and core of the tomatoes and cut them in half equatorially. Slice a thin round off the top or bottom (depending) of the tomato halves so that they easily sit up.

Place on a baking sheet. Brush the surface with olive oil. Then sprinkle on the dried herbs, the minced garlic (if you are using it), and the salt and pepper.

Bake for 15–20 minutes until hot and slightly softened.

Put on the fresh basil right before serving.

Spinach with Strawberries

Here is one of my nouvelle renditions of spinach. Not only is this a gorgeous dish (if I may say so), but the spinach tartness and the strawberry sweetness complement each other perfectly.

2 bunches spinach, washed and cut into 1-inch sections
1 cup strawberries, washed and stemmed
chives or finely sliced green onions to garnish

Serves 4

Melt a small amount of butter in a large skillet. Add all the spinach (or as much as you can fit in the pan), cover, and let cook 1–2 minutes. Stir the spinach, adding any you could not fit in at first. Cover and continue steaming until all the spinach has softened.

Halve or quarter the larger strawberries and set aside a few berries for garnish. Add the remaining berries at the very last instant, so that they heat briefly in the pan with the spinach.

Serve the spinach garnished with the reserved berries and some chives or green onion.

Variation: Try this with red chard (instead of the spinach) and strawberries.

Peas, Snowpeas & Blueberries

Here is another example of what happens if I am left to my own devices. You might consider this to be haphazard, but I would not put blueberries in with spinach; with peas and snowpeas, yes. A fun vegetable dish.

1 pound fresh peas
½ pound snowpeas
1 cup blueberries
a bit of butter, if you wish

Serves 4

Shell the peas, stem and string the snowpeas, and pick through the berries for stems, green berries, and overripe berries.

Drop the peas and snowpeas into boiling, salted water. They will be done in just about 3 minutes. Just before you drain them, drop in the blueberries. Give them about 10 seconds and then drain (reserving the cooking liquid for stock).

Toss in a pat of butter or leave plain, as you will.

Entrées With A Crust

HEAVEN AND HELL
(Adapted from a Japanese folk tale)

Contrary to popular belief
the tables of Hell are laden
with the most exquisite dishes of food.
Whatever you could possibly desire:
soups, salads, stews, sauces, curries
if you want, fruits, succulent meats
(grilled to order), pastries, ice cream.
The single unusual factor being that
one must eat with a fork three feet long.
Holding it close to the tines you could manage
to eat, but when you do so, a demon immediately
slaps you (or pokes you with his fork),
and says, "Hold it at the other end!"
So getting the food on the fork up to your mouth
is quite impossible, alas, though an abundance
of delicious food is readily available.

In heaven the situation is exactly the same:
same long tables covered with tasty dishes,
same long forks. The only difference in heaven
is that the people feed the person sitting
across the table from them.

Entrées With A Crust

The entrées with a crust are also entrées with cheese: pizzas and cheese pies—all dishes that have a festive, fun, and celebratory feeling. And, it turns out, these down-home beauties are fairly simple to prepare. (Even I can make them!)

The pizzas go from All-American (minus the meat) to Mexican and nouvelle California (throw in some goat cheese and zucchini). There is also a wonderful calzone, a fold-over pizza (again, minus the meat, but I must say it never occurs to me, "Where is the meat?" when I am eating).

What is known as "quiche" in some circles, we call "pie" or "tart." I cannot remember why we took up this form of inverse snobbery. Maybe it is so we would not be labeled "quiche-eaters." In any case, these recipes are devised to have particular flavor impact, whether it is from cumin seed, smoked cheese, or mustard.

AT HOME, AT LAST

Rolling out this dough
I take the air out of my sails
and float calmly on the seas,
not knowing how
things will turn out.

At last it is okay to be here.

Rolling, folding, turning, shaping,
seeing, smelling, touching, tasting,
Buoyantly I abide in this making
of food, this ceaseless labor
of feeding.

I make myself at home
in a universe
not of my choosing.

A Very Large Pizza

Planning to make pizza for 250–275 people?

For the dough:
24 *pounds whole wheat flour*
40 *pounds white flour*
2 *pounds rye flour*
1 *cup salt*

12 *cups fruity olive oil*
40 *cups milk*
40 *cups water*
2 *cups yeast*

Get that together!

For the sauce:
3 *gallons yellow onions*
3 *cups garlic*
3–4 *cups olive oil for sautéing*
8 *gallons pear tomatoes, drained,*
  seeded, chopped
1½–2 *gallons tomato paste*

4 *bottles red wine*
generous handfuls of dried herbs:
  basil, parsley, oregano, and
  marjoram
small handful anise seed

Cook that up!

To top it off:
6–8 *cups garlic oil*
36 *pounds mozzarella, grated*
20 *pounds Parmesan, grated*
enough other cheeses to make
  another 18 gallons
3 *gallons red onions, thinly*
  sliced quarter-moons
35 *pounds mushrooms, sliced*

5 *gallons bell peppers, sliced*
4 *gallons green or black olives,*
  sliced or chopped
30 *pounds fresh tomatoes, sliced*
  in rounds or half-rounds
6 *cups fresh herbs, chopped*
  (parsley, basil, marjoram,
  oregano)

Spread it on! Make a splash! Designer pizzas!
Paint with food!

Pizza Dough

Our version of pizza dough uses whole wheat and rye flour as well as white.

1 teaspoon dry yeast
⅓ cup warm water
good pinch of sugar
2 tablespoons rye flour
⅜ cup whole wheat flour
¾ cup white flour
½ teaspoon salt
⅙ cup milk
2 teaspoons olive oil
flour for kneading

Makes 2 8-inch pizzas

Dissolve the yeast in the warm water (less than 115°) with the sugar. Set aside in a warm place until the mixture turns bubbly, about 10 minutes.

Combine the flours and salt in a mixing bowl. Add the yeast mixture, milk, and olive oil. Stir until the ingredients come together in a rough dough.

Turn the dough out onto a lightly floured board and knead until smooth, adding flour as necessary to keep the dough from sticking.

Clean the bowl, coat it with a little olive oil, and return the kneaded dough to the bowl. Turn the dough over once so the upper surface is coated with oil. Cover with a dry towel.

Let the dough rise in a warm place for about 30 minutes or until doubled in size.

Turn out onto a floured board, knead briefly, and divide in 2 pieces. Roll out or stretch each piece into a circle 8 inches in diameter. (The rolling out or stretching is easier if the dough sits a few minutes after division.)

Place on heavy baking sheets or on individual pizza tins.

Goat Cheese Zucchini Pizza

Goat cheese has come a long way to have made it to a Buddhist meditation center in the California wilderness. We are up on the latest fads—
the edible ones anyway. A wonderful combination of flavors makes this
pizza disappear fast.

pizza dough (page 124)
3 tablespoons fruity olive oil
1 clove garlic
2 medium or 1 large tomato, sliced equatorially
1 cup zucchini, finely grated, salted, pressed
½ cup red onions, thinly sliced
1½ cups mozzarella cheese
1 cup goat cheese
½ cup basil, sliced in thin fine ribbons (chiffonade)
salt & pepper

Makes 2 8-inch pizzas
Preheat oven to 400°

Roll out pizza dough.

Mix the oil and garlic together. Brush generously on the pizza dough,
saving some to brush on top after baking.

Lay the tomato slices on the oiled dough.

Squeeze the zucchini in a cheesecloth or a clean dish towel to remove
excess liquid. Spread the zucchini over the tomatoes. (The zucchini,
finely grated, has been lightly salted, then placed in a bowl or colander,
with some weight on top of it. The salt and pressure draw water out of
the vegetable. It's then squeezed as dry as possible.)

Separate the red onion slices and spread over the zucchini.

Spread the mozzarella evenly over the vegetables.

Dot the goat cheese over the mozzarella.

Bake in preheated 400° oven for 15–20 minutes or until the crust is
brown. You can use a metal spatula to check the underside of the pizza.

Remove from the oven. Brush lightly with the garlic oil, especially
around the rim. Sprinkle with basil. Lightly salt and pepper.

Pizza Mexicana

This recipe is originally from Greens, our restaurant in San Francisco. Hot, spicy, well-seasoned, it is definitely pizza, but not one you'll find in Italy.

Chilpotle chili peppers are jalapenos which have been dried and smoked. Very hot and very tasty, they are available in cans. There is no real substitute for chilpotle peppers, but some alternatives are listed.

pizza dough (page 124)
¼ cup chilpotle "purée" (see instructions), OR *hot sauce,* OR *ketchup spiked with Tabasco,* OR *a layer of Ortega diced green chilis*
¾ cup Muenster cheese, grated
¾ cup Cheddar cheese, grated
½ cup Jack cheese, grated
1 small red onion, sliced into thin rounds
2 ripe tomatoes, cored at the top and sliced equatorially
1 red or green bell pepper, cored, seeded, and sliced into thin rounds
1 tablespoon olive oil
1 clove garlic, finely minced or pressed
pepper, freshly grated
2 teaspoons fresh marjoram, minced
2 teaspoons fresh cilantro, minced
1 ounce Parmesan cheese, freshly grated
additional olive oil

Makes 2 8-inch pizzas
Preheat oven to 400°

Roll out the pizza dough.

To make the chilpotle purée, take one chilpotle pepper and mince or purée very finely. Thin to spreading consistency by mixing in olive oil.

Spread the purée evenly over the pizza rounds.

Sprinkle the Muenster, Cheddar, and Jack cheeses on top of the purée.

Arrange the onions, tomatoes, and peppers on top of the cheese.

Combine the olive oil and garlic. Drizzle it over the vegetables.

Bake the pizza in the upper ⅓ of a preheated 400° oven for 15–20 minutes, or until the crust is brown and crisp around the edges.

Remove from the oven, sprinkle with the herbs and Parmesan cheese, and brush the edges of the crust with olive oil.

Serve immediately with cool liquid refreshment handy.

Tassajara Calzone

The recipe for this foldover pizza originally came to us from our friends at Chez Panisse. Ours doesn't have any meat (what's that?), but smoked cheese gives it a "cured" flavor and the vegetables provide something to bite into. This is such a succulent, juicy, flavorful pizza, how could anything be better, except as a little change of pace once in a while. After all, if you eat the same thing all the time, it begins to taste like brown rice. Here, there's something new in each bite.

For the filling:
1 small red onion, finely chopped
4 cloves garlic, minced
olive oil
1½ cups ricotta cheese
½ cup feta or goat cheese, crumbled
½ cup smoked cheese, Jack, or Gruyere, grated
½ cup Parmesan or asiago cheese, grated
1 tablespoon herbs (thyme, rosemary, marjoram, basil), freshly
  chopped, OR *½ tablespoon dried herbs*
up to 1½ cups any combination of:
  zucchini, grated, salted, pressed, squeezed (see Zucchini Goat Cheese
  Pizza)
  carrots, peeled, grated, or finely chopped
  olives, green or black, pitted, sliced, or chopped
  sun-dried tomatoes, small dice or strips
salt & black pepper

For one calzone: serves 1–6
Preheat oven to 425°

Sauté the onions and garlic in olive oil until the onions are soft. If fresh herbs are not available, add the dried herbs to the cooking onions. (The fresh herbs are added uncooked later.)

Mix the cooked onions and garlic with the cheeses, the raw vegetables, the olives and tomatoes, and the fresh herbs. Salt and black pepper to taste.

For assembly:
Pizza dough for 2 8-inch pizzas (page 124)
2 tablespoons olive oil
1 small clove garlic, pressed or minced

Roll out dough into a circle about 12 inches in diameter and place it on a cookie sheet lined with baking paper or foil.

Combine garlic and oil. Brush the dough with the garlic oil, leaving 1-inch rim unoiled. Brush this rim with water. Place the filling on one half of the oiled dough and fold over the other half to make the calzone.

Pinch the rims together and then fold the rims in half to seal. Crimp the sealed edges with a fork. Poke the surface all over with a fork to make air holes. (Yes, even calzone needs to breathe.)

Brush the dough with egg wash (page 35). Decorate with herb leaves if you wish (flat sage leaves work well). Brush more eggwash over the leaves so they will remain in place.

Bake at 425° for about 25 minutes or until golden brown.

Serve whole to enjoy its beauty. Then, cut into slices.

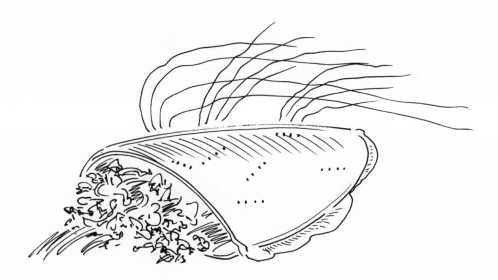

All-American 4th of July Pizza

At Tassajara we celebrate the 4th of July with a big feast and party. In addition to our usual guests and residents, we invite our neighbors from down the road—fourteen miles, an hour's drive down the road—and over 100 make the trip.

Here is our version of All-American pizza. Jeffrey has made it the last four years, and he has been kind enough to divulge some of his secrets.

For the sauce:

2 large yellow onions, cut into quarter moon slices
8 (or more depending on your capacity) large cloves garlic, chopped
fruity olive oil for sautéing
salt
¼–½ teaspoon each of any or

all of the following dried herbs: parsley, basil, thyme, oregano, marjoram
large pinch dried whole anise seed
2 cups (or so) decent red wine
8 ounces tomato purée
4 ounces tomato paste

Makes 2 pizzas
Preheat oven to 400°

Sauté the onions and garlic in the olive oil in a heavy-bottomed saucepan over high heat for a couple of minutes.

Reduce the heat to medium and add a touch of salt, the dried herbs (the smaller amounts to start with), the anise seed, and ½ cup of the red wine. Allow to cook thoroughly until the onions are quite soft.

Add the tomato purée and paste, thinning if need be with the rest of the wine.

Allow this mixture to cook on a low flame for a lengthy time, adding wine as needed to keep it from becoming too thick.

When you can see preparation in sight, begin tasting for salt and herbs.

Start the pizza dough (see page 124) about 1–1½ hours before final assembly to give it time to rise. (We start ours hours ahead and keep it in large plastic barrels in the walk-in refrigerator, bringing it out in time to warm up, divide up, and shape into pizzas.)

For assembly:

pizza dough for 2 8-inch pizzas
½ cup garlic oil (allow a coarsely chopped clove of garlic to steep in ½ cup olive oil)
1 cup mozzarella, grated
½ cup Parmesan, grated
1 cup your choice of cheese (Cheddar, smoked, Jack . . .), grated
1 small red onion, thinly sliced in half moons
1 bell pepper (green, red, or yellow), thinly sliced strips or rings
¾ cup green or black olives, chopped or sliced
1½ cups mushrooms, sliced into "little trees"
a fresh tomato, sliced into half or quarter moons
½ cup fresh herbs (parsley, basil, thyme, oregano, marjoram or what-have-you), minced
salt & pepper

Roll out the pizza dough and brush with the garlic oil (reserving some for brushing on after baking).

Smooth on the sauce and then the cheeses.

Arrange whichever combo of toppings you have decided to use: onions, peppers, olives, mushrooms, tomatoes.

Pop into the oven preheated to 400° (upper shelf). Bake for 15–20 minutes, or until the crust is brown and crisp around the edges.

Remove from the oven and brush immediately with more garlic oil. Sprinkle on the fresh herbs and finish with a couple shakes of salt and grinds of pepper.

Voilà!

Cheese Pie Dough

This dough, when well-prepared, is flaky, tender, and buttery. We prefer it to doughs made with shortening or oil, though the use of butter requires special attention. The little lumps of butter provide the flake, so it is essential that the butter remain cold and lumpy throughout the process, that it does not become so soft that it mixes in *with* the flour and water. As you can see in the recipe, this is accomplished in various ways: using chilled or frozen butter, using ice water, mixing lightly, and freezing before baking. The procedure before baking takes some time, but the finished pie will be flakier and shapelier for the effort.

1 cup plus 2 tablespoons white pastry flour
¼ teaspoon salt
⅓ cup sweet butter
3–4 tablespoons cold water (preferably ice water)

Makes 1 cheese pie

Mix the flour and the salt. Cut in the butter with a pastry knife. (Or, as Jeffrey prefers, freeze the butter beforehand and grate it into the flour.) The mixture will look like coarse cornmeal in color and texture.

Add the cold water, a tablespoon at a time, using only enough to allow the mixture to come together and form a ball. Excess water will make the dough tougher. Mix either with a fork or with the hands, handling the dough as little as possible, but using some pressure to bring the dough together.

Wrap the dough in wax paper and a plastic bag, if not using it immediately. The dough will last a week or longer in the freezer.

To reduce shrinkage in baking, roll the dough out and let it "rest" in the refrigerator for about ½ hour before shaping it into the pie pan.

Shape the chilled dough into the pie pan. Freeze the shaped dough hard (about 1 hour) before baking it. If baking without a filling, preheat oven to 375° and then put the dough into the oven while still frozen. (We usually keep some dried beans around for filling the pie shell to keep it from expanding and sagging during baking.) Bake about 20–25 minutes until lightly browned.

132

Jack Cheese & Onion Tart with Cumin Seeds

Mild cheese accented with well-roasted onions and cumin, this dish sings sweet and pungent. Cream added to the eggs makes the custard smooth, fine-textured, and rich. If you prefer, however, you can use all milk.

a pre-baked pie or tart shell (see page 132)
1 yellow onion, thinly sliced
1 tablespoon butter
2 teaspoons freshly ground cumin seeds, pulverized in a spice mill
boiling water
3 eggs

½ teaspoon salt
½ cup milk
1 cup cream (or more milk)
⅔ cup grated Monterey Jack cheese
1 teaspoon whole cumin seeds
coarsely ground fresh black pepper

Makes 1 9-inch tart
Preheat oven to 375°

Cook the onions slowly in the butter with the ground cumin until soft and thoroughly cooked, about 25 minutes.

Add a few spoonfuls of boiling water from time to time to facilitate the cooking and prevent the cumin from burning. The onions should be nicely caramelized, brown, and sweet.

Whisk the eggs and salt until light, then add the milk and cream and whisk to combine.

Spread the cheese in the pre-baked shell, then layer with the onions and scatter the whole cumin seeds on top. Sprinkle with pepper to taste.

Pour the egg mixture on top.

Bake in the upper third of a preheated 375° oven until the custard is set and the top is golden, about 40 minutes.

Remove the tart to a rack and let cool 5–10 minutes before serving. This allows the flavors time to develop.

Tassajara Smoked Cheese & Spinach Pie

Adapting an old favorite, we have added smoked cheese to give this pie a flavor reminiscent of bacon. The spinach lends a contrasting color and flavor.

1 uncooked pie shell (see page 132)
Dijon mustard
½ cup grated Cheddar cheese
½ cup grated Parmesan cheese (or asiago or Romano)
½ cup smoked cheese
1 small bunch spinach (about 2 cups washed and cut), OR ½ package frozen spinach, thawed

1 cup mushrooms, sliced
3 eggs
½ cup milk
½ cup cream (or an additional ½ cup milk)
Tabasco sauce (optional)

Note: If you do not happen to have mushrooms, add an additional egg and another ¼ cup each of milk and cream to the custard.

Makes 1 9-inch pie
Preheat oven to 425°

Brush the uncooked pie shell generously with the Dijon mustard and sprinkle the cheeses evenly over the mustard.

Cut the stems off the leaves of spinach, and slice the leaves in strips ¼-inch wide.

Sauté the mushrooms over moderate heat for 3–4 minutes and add the spinach. Continue cooking until the spinach has softened. Spread the mushrooms and spinach on top of the cheese.

Beat the eggs in a bowl and whisk in the milk, cream, and a touch of Tabasco. (You can use all milk, if you prefer.) Pour over the vegetables.

Bake for 15 minutes at 425°, then lower the heat to 300°. Continue baking for 25–30 minutes, until a knife inserted in the center comes out clean.

Remove from the oven and let stand 5 minutes before slicing.

Cheddar Pie with Mustard & Chives

This is a light, custardy pie, flavorful with mustard, cheese, and herbs—
a handsome golden pie flecked with green.

a pre-baked pie shell (page 132)
1 tablespoon good mustard, coarse or fine
1½ cups grated sharp Cheddar cheese
1 cup cream
1 cup milk
¼ teaspoon salt
4 eggs
½ teaspoon dried dill or 1 tablespoon chopped fresh dill
¼ cup sliced chives or scallions (green and white scallion rings)

Makes 1 9-inch pie
Preheat oven to 400°

Spread the mustard over the bottom of the crust, then cover with the
grated cheese.

Whisk the cream, milk, salt, and eggs together until well-blended, then
stir in the herbs.

Pour the mixture evenly over the cheese.

Bake the pie in the upper third of a preheated 400° oven for 10 minutes,
then reduce the temperature to 300° and bake for another 25 minutes,
or until the top is golden, the custard is set, and a knife comes out clean
when inserted in the center.

Remove the pie to a rack and let stand for 10 minutes before serving.

Tofu Entrées

FEEDING ALL (WITHOUT STRESS)

Who breathes an enjoyable breath
while hard at work knows riches
that money does not bring. Yet
we knot our breath and work
under stress. What hunger is this
we feed?
If we were to eat half as much meat,
drink half as much liquor, then
everyone could eat well, worldwide.
Yet we feed the stress we build,
and overlook the price we pay.
Animals we pen and cage: no
fields for these four legs, no
earth to peck, no dawn of day, no
dawdling in midday heat, no rest
of darkness. What kind of life
is this? They too grow stress,
impulse to move and graze is caged,
all this pent-up in meat we eat,
yet we do the same to ourselves,
battling to succeed.
May we let up, step in open space,
free from our own imprisoning,
making wise and proper use of structure,
fulfilling heart's desire.

Tofu Entrées

"Tofu" is the Japanese name for bean curd, and, over the last ten years, it has come a long way: all the way into the supermarkets and even some corner groceries (at least in the San Francisco Bay Area). As you will see in the recipes, tofu has also been adapted to Western cuisine. What started out in miso soup and vegetable stir-fries has gotten into gumbo and stroganoff. High protein, low calorie, easy to digest, tofu can be prepared in a number of delicious and satisfying ways.

All of the recipes use "firm" rather than "soft" tofu (soft will not hold together in cooking). Most of the recipes call for the tofu to be "drained and pressed." The idea here is to remove from the tofu any excess liquid; this allows it to hold together better in cooking and to absorb flavors better. This is done by cutting the block of tofu into three or four slabs of equal thickness and placing these on a slanting surface, usually a cutting board or baking tray. Another cutting board or tray placed on top of the tofu applies a slight pressure to help squeeze out the liquid. Let the tofu drain for 20–30 minutes, if you have the time. Then it is ready to go.

Tofu Marinade

This marinade is the secret ingredient for unblanding tofu. We use this recipe to marinate tofu before charcoal-grilling it at our restaurant, Greens, in San Francisco. As Tassajara we use it for the Grilled Marinated Tofu.

2 blocks of tofu
½ ounce dried mushrooms
1 cup water
2 teaspoons dried oregano
2 cloves garlic, pressed or pounded
½ cup fruity olive oil
½ cup sherry wine vinegar OR *red wine vinegar*
½ cup red wine
½ cup soy sauce (tamari, if possible)
pinch ground cloves
½ teaspoon salt
some twists of black pepper

Makes enough to marinate 2 blocks of tofu

Drain and press the tofu (see page 139) to remove excess water.

Simmer the mushrooms in the water for 15 minutes.

Toast the oregano in a small frying pan over a medium flame until it becomes aromatic (without burning).

Combine the remaining ingredients, adding the oregano when it is ready. Then combine with the simmering mushrooms.

Bring to a boil and simmer a couple minutes longer.

Cut the tofu into four slabs.

Pour the hot marinade over the tofu slabs. Marinate for at least 2 hours, preferably overnight (refrigerate). The tofu can marinate several days. If the tofu was reasonably fresh and fairly dry when it was marinated, the marinade can be boiled, strained, and kept refrigerated for reuse.

Grilled Marinated Tofu

Once the tofu has been marinated—at least a day—this dish is simple and quick to prepare. As you can see from the variation, sesame oil is not essential; the dish can be flavored in a variety of ways.

1 block of tofu marinated for at least 1 day (see page 141 for Tofu
*   Marinade)*
light and dark sesame oil
2 medium yellow onions, sliced
½ pound mushrooms, sliced
tamari sauce
salt & pepper
2 cloves garlic, finely minced
boiling water
breadcrumbs, flour, or cornmeal

Yields 4 servings

Remove the tofu from the marinade and drain it on a slanted board (see page 139) while you slice and cook the mushrooms and onions.

Heat about 2 teaspoons of both oils in a large skillet.

Add the onions to the hot oil and sauté over high heat until they begin to brown. Add the mushrooms, sauté another few minutes, then add a tablespoon of tamari and immediately turn down the heat. Add salt and pepper and the garlic.

Add the boiling water in small increments when the pan seems dry, so that the water immediately bubbles and begins to reduce, leaving a glaze as it does so. Continue adding and reducing until the onions and mushrooms are cooked, then set them aside on a warm plate.

Add another few teaspoons of both oils to the skillet.

Cut the tofu into fork-size chunks. Coat the chunks with crumbs or flour or cornmeal and roast in the hot oil until the tofu is warm inside and brown outside.

Add the onions and mushrooms and make sure everything is hot before serving. It can be kept hot, or can finish heating, in the oven if you have other preparations to make.

Garnish with green onions.

Variation: Use the same ingredients and method as above but use a light and fruity olive oil instead of the sesame oils and some fresh marjoram and thyme with the onions and/or in the breading. The flavor will be completely different. Serve with freshly grated Parmesan cheese.

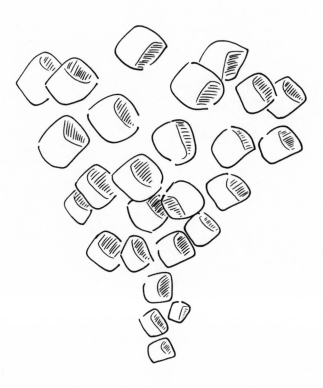

Tofu Cutlets

No longer does tofu have to be bland and plain! Here's a dish that makes a substantial, flavorful, appealing meal of tofu. Be sure to use *firm* tofu; the softer varieties will tend to fall apart.

1½ (24 ounces) blocks firm tofu
1½ teaspoons dried thyme
1 teaspoon dried savory
2 teaspoons dried basil
2 teaspoons dried marjoram
1 cup breadcrumbs, lightly toasted in the oven
1 cup Parmesan cheese, finely grated
½ teaspoon salt
black pepper, a generous grinding
2 eggs
safflower or other light oil for frying
lemon wedges, for garnish
basil-flavored tartar sauce (page 96)

Serves 4

Press and drain the tofu.

Crush the herbs between your fingers or in your palms to release their fragrance. Combine them with the breadcrumbs, cheese, salt, and pepper in a pie plate.

Break the eggs into another pie plate and beat lightly with a fork.

Slice the drained tofu into strips or squares about ½-inch thick and 3 inches long. (½-inch × ½-inch × 3-inch for strips, ½-inch × 3-inch × 3-inch for squares.)

Heat the oil (a good ⅛-inch) in a large, heavy skillet until the surface shimmers, (350° on a deep-fry thermometer). Adjust the heat to medium-low so the temperature does not rise higher.

Dip the pieces of tofu in the egg, then into the crumbs, coating both sides thoroughly. Dip the same piece twice in the egg, then the crumbs, for heavier breading.

Fry the coated tofu in the oil until browned on both or all four sides, about 2–3 minutes per side, then drain on paper toweling.

Serve immediately with slices of lemon and a basil-flavored tartar sauce.

Some additional notes: Prior to frying, the breaded tofu can be arranged on a plate or in a pan, so you can finish the breading before you start the frying. Also, when you have other last minute preparations, the fried tofu sticks can be placed in a casserole dish and kept warm in the oven prior to serving.

As a variation, add ¼ cup of cornmeal in place of breadcrumbs.

Tofu Teriyaki

This casserole with bright flavors and aromas is simple to prepare, but the tofu needs to be marinated a day ahead of time. Since the dish is fairly juicy, it is excellent served over plain rice or noodles.

Serves 4–6

For the teriyaki marinade:
1 cup soy sauce
½ cup sake or white wine
*½ cup sugar (*OR *part honey)*
1 tablespoon fresh ginger, grated
6 cloves garlic, crushed or pressed
¼ cup sesame oil
1½ teaspoons dry mustard

Combine all the ingredients in a saucepan and heat to boiling, then simmer for 10 minutes.

To marinate the tofu:
2 blocks of firm tofu
teriyaki marinade

Cut the tofu blocks in half and drain the excess water from the tofu by placing it on a slanted surface, either a cutting board or one end of a baking pan.

Let the tofu drain for 20–30 minutes, then cut it in approximately 1-inch × 1-inch × 2-inch chunks.

Pour the hot marinade over the tofu and let it marinate overnight. Once the mixture has cooled, place it in the refrigerator.

For the casserole:
the marinated tofu
2 medium-large onions, cut in quarter moons
2 bell peppers, cut in strips
2 cups mushroom halves
6 medium tomatoes OR *4 large tomatoes, cut in wedges*
1 scallion for garnish, thinly sliced

Sauté the onions for 1–2 minutes, then add the peppers and continue sautéing for about 5 minutes. Remove from the pan. Drain and reserve the liquid.

Sauté the mushrooms for 3–4 minutes. Remove, drain, and reserve the liquid.

To assemble the casserole:

Layer tofu, onion-peppers, tomatoes, tofu, onion-peppers, mushrooms, tomatoes.

Combine the reserved juice from the onions and peppers and mushrooms with an equal or greater amount of the teriyaki marinade and add it to the casserole. Add at least ½ cup altogether.

Bake uncovered at 350° about 45 minutes, until heated through.

Sprinkle on the sliced scallions to garnish and cover during the last 5 minutes of baking.

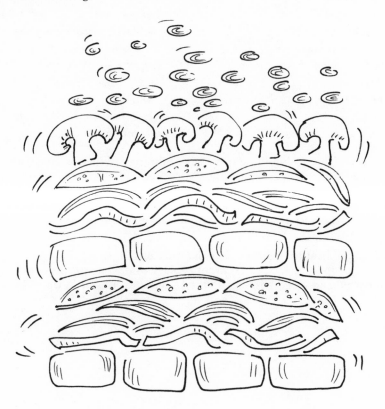

Eleanor's Tofu Gumbo

It was simply a matter of time until tofu was turned into gumbo: Creole cooking works its wonders with the blob of the East. A bit of work, a bit of patience, a bit of tending is needed. We served this with corn bread, a green salad with avocado and grapefruit slices, and pecan pie.

The recipe is in two parts: a roux and a gumbo, which are eventually combined. Some ingredients are used in both, so you can, for instance, cut the peppers at the same time.

Another point to keep in mind: if, at any time, you discover the gumbo has burned or scorched the bottom of the pot, transfer it to another pot. This will keep the burnt smell from permeating the gumbo.

Serves 4–6

For the roux:

½ cup butter
¾ cup flour
1 medium yellow onion, diced
½ red bell pepper, slivered or
  diced
½ green bell pepper, slivered or
  diced
1 stalk celery, sliced

large pinch salt
⅛–¼ teaspoon cayenne pepper
⅛–¼ teaspoon white pepper
¼ teaspoon black pepper
2 cloves garlic, pressed or
  pounded
½ teaspoon each dried thyme,
  marjoram, and oregano

Heat the butter to bubbling in a heavy-bottomed skillet or saucepan. Add the flour, stirring vigorously. Cook over high heat, stirring swiftly and continuously, until the roux becomes a very dark brown, similar in color to chocolate. This will take about 15 minutes. (Eleanor says it is very important to keep the flame up all the way and to scrape the bottom constantly!)

Reduce the heat to medium after the roux has darkened. Add the onions, peppers, celery, salt, cayenne, black and white peppers, garlic, and herbs, and cook, stirring, about 15 minutes. It's thick, right? Set aside.

For the gumbo:

½ cup butter

1½ pounds okra, caps removed
and sliced in ½-inch rounds

2 ears of corn, cut the kernels off
the cob and scrape the cob for
pulp

1 large yellow onion, sliced

½ red bell pepper, slivered or
diced

½ green bell pepper, slivered or
diced

1 stalk celery, sliced

6 cloves garlic, finely minced

salt, good sprinkling

¼ teaspoon cayenne pepper

¼ teaspoon white pepper

⅛–¼ teaspoon black pepper

2 1-pound cans tomatoes,
drained and diced large

3 cups stock or water

1 block (16 ounces) tofu, pressed
and drained, cut into small
cubes

Start the stock simmering, if you are going to use a stock. The variation on Oriental Stock (page 67) can be used. Use the drained liquid from the canned tomatoes, if you like, instead.

Drain and press the tofu (see page 139).

Heat the butter until bubbling, add the okra and cook, stirring often. The okra will begin to ooze its juices ("and look vile," according to our Mississippi-born chef). Continue cooking and stirring over medium to high heat for about 35 minutes. The okra will be stringy, sort of like medium mozzarella. The point of the cooking is to get the okra to emit its juices and dry out some.

Add the corn. Continue cooking and stirring over high heat another 5–10 minutes.

Add the onions, the bell peppers, celery, garlic, and salt. Do not leave the pot; keep stirring and stirring—especially the bottom to keep the vegetables from sticking and burning.

Add the peppers. Cook, stirring (!) over high heat until the mixture is quite dry.

Add the tomatoes and stew over moderate heat 5–10 minutes.

Mix in the roux. Add stock to desired consistency and/or volume. (The gumbo can sit at this point, off the heat, to be reheated, slowly, before serve-up. Add the tofu to the sitting gumbo so that it can absorb the flavors.)

Add the tofu. Check seasoning and serve.

Pass gumbo file ("available at any ol' grocery store in the gourmet section") at the table to sprinkle on the gumbo.

Tofu Miso Stew

This can be a hearty, satisfying, one-bowl meal in itself. Or, it can be served with brown or white rice, or buckwheat noodles. Or, it could be accompanied with a green salad.

Preparation is in three parts: the stock, the vegetables for stewing, and the sauce. Although it may appear complicated on paper, one step leads to another and the whole dish is completed in about an hour.

The dark sesame oil called for provides a smokey, nutty flavor, but the dish can be made without it. It is available at natural food stores, Japanese or Chinese markets, and some supermarkets.

Miso is a bean paste (with high protein content) made from soy beans. Excellent as a seasoning, it has been making its appearance in some supermarkets, as well as in Asian food markets and natural food stores.

Do not think you must include all the vegetables—five or six will do.
Note: the amounts for the vegetables are approximate.

For the stock:

Make the Oriental Stock (page 67). After 20 minutes, pull out the dried mushrooms, remove the tough stems (if any), cut the caps into thick slices or quarters, and set them aside.

To begin the stew:

2 *medium onions, cut in wedges*

2 *tablespoons dark sesame oil (or soy, or what-have-you)*

3 *medium carrots, peeled and roll-cut into 1-inch pieces*

2 *celery ribs, cut on the diagonal into ½-inch pieces*

6-*inch piece of gobo (burdock root), scrubbed well and roll-cut, or matchsticks (not essential)*

2 *cups fresh mushrooms, halved, quartered, or left whole, if small*

1 *yam (about 1½ cups), cut into quarters lengthwise and then into ½-inch sections*

1 *cup turnip or daikon, cut like the yam*

1 *medium potato (about 1 cup), scrubbed and cut like the yam*

5 *cloves garlic, coarsely minced*

1 *inch of fresh ginger, finely grated*

Cook the onions in the sesame oil in a large, heavy-bottomed stew pot over moderate-high heat. Stir frequently and continue cooking until they start to brown, about 8–10 minutes.

Add the remaining vegetables, garlic, ginger, and the reserved mushrooms (if you were using them) from the stock. Stir to coat evenly with a thin film of oil.

Salt lightly, cover with a tight-fitting lid, then reduce the heat to low. Check occasionally to make sure there is enough liquid in the bottom of the pot so that the vegetables do not burn. Add a little stock or water if necessary.

Proceed to make the sauce.

For the sauce:
¼ cup barley flour (whole wheat or white)
5 tablespoons dark sesame oil
2½ cups of the stock
5 tablespoons red miso mixed with ½ cup stock
soy sauce to taste

Toast the barley flour in a dry saucepan over moderate heat until fragrant, shaking the pan or stirring frequently to prevent scorching.

Add the sesame oil, stir to blend thoroughly, and then slowly whisk in the stock.

Simmer 10 minutes, stirring occasionally to produce a medium-thick sauce.

Remove from heat and add the diluted miso. Season with soy sauce.

Add the sauce to the stewing vegetables and stir gently to combine. The stew may seem somewhat dry at this point, but the vegetables should continue to release their juices as they cook.

Return lid to the pot and continue to simmer on low heat.

To complete the stew:

3 tablespoons each dark and light sesame oil

1 block firm tofu, pressed and drained (page 139), cut into ½-inch
cubes

4–6 scallions, including the crisp green tops, cut into 2-inch lengths

fresh cilantro

Chinese pepper (Szechwan pepper) OR *black pepper*

Heat 2 tablespoons of each oil in a skillet or wok until hot. Add the tofu and sauté over moderate heat until lightly golden.

Combine the tofu with the stewing vegetables.

Add the remaining oil to the skillet and sauté the scallions just until their fragrance blooms.

Stir them gently into the stew, taking care not to break the tofu.

Continue cooking until all the vegetables are tender, perhaps another 10 minutes.

Garnish with cilantro and Chinese pepper. If you can get it, the Chinese pepper is exquisitely aromatic. Otherwise, make use of what you have.

Alaskan Tofu

The student who came up with this recipe came down from Alaska, hence the name. The flavors, however, are closer to Provence or Japan.

Serves 4
Preheat oven to 350°

1 16-ounce block of tofu, pressed to remove excess water (page 139)
1½ cups yellow onions, thinly sliced
1 tablespoon olive oil
1 cup sliced red bell peppers
2 healthy pinches each of dried marjoram and thyme, OR a tablespoon or more of chopped fresh herbs

1 – 1½ cups sliced mushrooms, ¼-inch thick
1½ cups coarsely grated fontina cheese
¾ cup pitted and chopped Greek olives
¼ cup minced red onion
1 cup diced green bell pepper

For the sauce:
2 tablespoons fruity olive oil
2 tablespoons sherry vinegar or Balsamic vinegar
2 tablespoons mirin (Japanese cooking wine) OR white wine

1 heaping tablespoon red miso
1 tablespoon tamari
1 teaspoon Dijon mustard
1 teaspoon pressed or pounded garlic

Cut the tofu into 1-inch cubes, layer in a heatproof casserole or baking pan, then bake in a preheated 350° oven for 20 minutes.

Drain any liquid released by the baking and set the tofu aside in the casserole. Leave the oven on.

Sauté the yellow onions in the olive oil over medium-high heat until lightly browned. Add the red peppers, herbs, and mushrooms. Stir to coat the mixture with a thin film of oil, then reduce the heat to low and let the vegetables cook undisturbed until soft.

Combine the sauce ingredients in a small bowl and add to the cooked vegetables. Cook briefly to heat through, then remove the pan from the heat.

Toss the cheese, olives, red onions, and green peppers in the casserole with the tofu.

Add the cooked vegetables and sauce and stir gently to mix.

Cover and return the casserole to the oven to bake until bubbling, about 30 minutes.

Serve with brown or white rice.

Mushroom Tofu Stroganoff

This juicy, succulent, satisfying tofu dish is one of our most popular offerings. Serve it over rice or egg noodles.

1 16-ounce block of tofu, pressed, drained (see introduction to tofu
　　dishes, page 139), and marinated (see page 141)
1 tablespoon olive oil
5 tablespoons butter
1 large yellow onion, diced medium-small
1 pound mushrooms (regular button, or part oyster mushrooms, or
　　fresh shiitake, if available)
2 teaspoons minced garlic
½ teaspoon paprika
1 teaspoon nutritional yeast
a pinch dried thyme (or ½ teaspoon of fresh thyme, minced)
1 tablespoon tamari or soy sauce
salt and freshly ground pepper
½ cup dry sherry or red wine
1 cup mushroom or vegetable stock
1½ cups sour cream

Serves 4
Preheat oven to 350°

Drain the marinated tofu on a slanted board while you gather and prepare the rest of the ingredients. Cut the tofu into strips or cubes and bake at 350° for 20 minutes or so. Remove and set aside.

Heat 1 tablespoon each olive oil and butter in a 12-inch sauté pan. When the oil/butter is hot, add the onions. Sauté them on a high heat until they begin to brown, then turn down the heat and cook the onions carefully until they begin to caramelize, stirring frequently. This will take about 15 minutes. They should be soft. While they are cooking, slice the mushrooms about ¼-inch thick, chop the garlic, and warm the stock.

Mix the garlic, paprika, nutritional yeast, and a pinch of dried thyme (or the ½ teaspoon of fresh minced thyme) into the cooked onions.

Add the remaining 4 tablespoons of butter and the tamari. When the butter is melted, add the mushrooms. Salt and pepper them and carefully stir. Once the mushrooms begin to cook, add the tofu and the sherry or wine, and let bubble and simmer for 8–10 minutes.

Add the heated stock to the sour cream. Once the mushrooms are sufficiently cooked, add the sour cream stock to the pan.

Cook until the sauce is hot and reduced to the thickness you want. Try not to boil the sauce for too long or the sour cream will curdle.

Check the seasonings and serve over rice or twisted egg noodles.

Other Favorite Entrées

AND STILL WE COOK

Any moment, preparing this meal,
we could be gas thirty thousand
feet in the air, soon
to fall out poisonous on leaf,
frond, and fur. Everything
in sight would cease.

And still we cook,
putting a thousand cherished
dreams on the table, to nourish
and reassure those close and dear.

In this act of cooking, I bid farewell.
Always I insisted you alone were to blame.
This last instant my eyes open
and I regard you with all
the tenderness and forgiveness
I withheld for so long.

With no future
we have nothing
to fight about.

May all beings be happy, healthy, free from suffering!

Other Favorite Entrées

This section, which includes those recipes that did not fit into the other entrée sections, is comprised of substantial dishes, not lacking in heft, flavor, or cheese (yes, even the pasta has a cheese garnish). These are not dishes to leave you feeling hungry, except for the most inveterate carnivore. Dig in!

When I look over the list, I see a wide assortment, including a couple of egg dishes, two polenta dishes, a pasta, a potato casserole, a moussaka, a tortilla casserole, and one of our instant "classics": Cheese and Nut Loaf. I can't help it, I am impressed: these people eat well . . . not bad for an isolated mountain Zen spa.

Yet, the true test is not my rambling thoughts, but your mouths and stomachs. How is it out there, Topeka?

Scalloped Potatoes with Smoked Cheese

These potatoes are complemented by a cool purée of apples and pears or, in the fall, quince. The combination of the smokey flavor, the richness of the cream, and the perfume of the quince, makes for a perfect autumn supper.

3 tablespoons butter
1 clove garlic, crushed under the broad side of a knife
1 cup Gruyere cheese, grated
½ cup smoked cheese, grated (smoked Gouda, smoked mozzarella, or
  Bruderbasil)
2 pounds russet (or red) potatoes
salt & freshly grated black pepper
2 cups milk
1 cup cream mixed with 1 tablespoon flour
½ cup breadcrumbs

Makes 6 servings
Preheat oven to 350°

Coat the bottom and sides of a shallow 3-quart casserole liberally with a tablespoon or so of the butter. Rub the garlic into the butter, then discard (unless you'd like to press it into the melted butter that is poured over the top later).

Combine the two cheeses.

Wash the potatoes, without peeling, and slice them into even rounds ⅛ inch thick. Arrange a layer of potatoes in the casserole, add salt, pepper, and half the cheese. Repeat once more, then finish with a layer of potatoes prettily overlapped on top. Salt and pepper the top layer.

Heat the milk and pour it over the potatoes, followed by the cream and flour mixture.

Scatter the breadcrumbs evenly over the surface. Melt the remaining butter (with the pressed garlic?), and drizzle it over the breadcrumbs. If breadcrumbs are too much of a chore (as they are for me sometimes) sprinkle on some grated Parmesan cheese in their place.

Bake in a preheated 350° oven until the cream and milk are absorbed and the potatoes are tender when pierced with a fork, about 1¼ hours.

Cheese & Nut Loaf

A vegetarian meat loaf, this dish is rich and filling, a well-loved dish even in the summertime. It is even better in cold weather, and its specialness makes it a dish that often appears at our Thanksgiving or Christmas dinners.

2 tablespoons butter or oil
1 onion, diced in ¼-inch pieces
1½ cups chopped mushrooms
2 cloves garlic, minced
1 small green pepper, cut into small squares
1 teaspoon each dried thyme, savory, and marjoram
½ teaspoon dried sage
salt & freshly ground pepper
1½ cups cooked brown rice

1½ cups walnuts, ground or finely chopped
½ cup cashews, ground or finely chopped
4 eggs
1 cup cottage cheese
¾ pound grated cheese: Cheddar, Gruyere, fontina, smoked, individually or in combination (no matter which you choose, include some Parmesan!)
¼ cup mixed fresh herbs, such as parsley, oregano, thyme

Makes 1 9-inch loaf
Preheat oven to 350°

Heat the butter or oil in a skillet and cook the onion until it begins to soften.

Add the mushrooms, garlic, green pepper, dried herbs, and a little salt and pepper. Then cook until the mushrooms and peppers are soft.

Place the cooked vegetables in a large bowl, add all the remaining ingredients, and mix well.

Check the seasoning. Leave it a bit undersalted at this point because the saltiness of the cheeses will become more apparent later.

Line the bottom and sides of a 9-inch bread pan with two crossed rectangles of baking parchment or foil, leaving about 3 inches overhanging on each side. Liberally butter the lined pan, including the ends.

Put the cheese and nut mixture in the pan, rap the pan sharply on a counter once or twice to get rid of air bubbles, then smooth out the top with a spatula or spoon.

Fold the overhanging paper over the top. Bake in a preheated 350° oven for about 1 hour, until firm to touch.

Remove the pan to a cooling rack and let it sit for 5–10 minutes. Pull the paper back from the top of the loaf, and turn it out onto a serving platter.

Garnish with vegetables, or tomatoes, or serve with yeast gravy and parsley. Perhaps some grated cheese over the top.

Serve with Nut Loaf Sauce (page 95), mushroom gravy, or a bechamel.

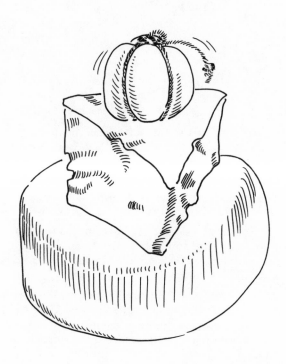

Spring Vegetable Timbale

Fresh vegetables baked in an egg and cheese custard, timbales have a surprising elegance. They are easy to prepare, yet sustaining and satisfying to eat. This one is bejeweled with many colors, which come into view once the timbale is sliced. We usually serve this with a sorrel sauce or vegetable bechamel.

1 large leek, primarily white part
  OR *1 medium onion*
butter, for cooking
¼ cup white wine
½ cup mushrooms, thinly sliced
salt & pepper
½ cup fresh peas
½ cup asparagus tips and thinly sliced stems
½ cup carrots, cut into matchsticks, then cubes

½ bunch spinach (about 1 cup)
1¼ cups milk or light cream
3 tablespoons butter
5 tablespoons dry breadcrumbs, made from white bread
5 eggs
½ teaspoon salt
white pepper
1 cup grated cheese, Gruyere or fontina

Makes 1 9-inch loaf (or equivalent)
Serves 4–6 people
Preheat oven to 325°

Slice, then dice the white part of the leek. Wash the pieces well to rid them of sand and then dry as you would lettuce. Cook slowly in butter until soft. The white wine can be added while the leeks are cooking, and reduced.

Remove the leeks, add another dollop of butter, and cook the mushrooms with a little salt and pepper on low heat until they are soft.

Blanch the peas, asparagus, and carrots in boiling salted water until they are barely cooked—still somewhat firm. Drain in a strainer set over a pot to save the cooking liquid. Rinse the vegetables in cold water to stop the cooking. Allow to drain, or dry on a towel.

Remove the stems from the spinach, cut the leaves into narrow strips, and blanch them briefly in the boiling salted water. Rinse in cool water and set aside to drain, squeezing most of the moisture out with your hands. The cooking liquid and the juices from the spinach can be saved for stock or soup.

Heat the milk or cream with the butter until it is melted and the milk is quite warm.

Prepare the loaf pan by buttering liberally and then lining with bread-crumbs (which are great, but not essential).

Beat the eggs with the salt and a touch of white pepper and gradually whisk in the milk. Add the vegetables and cheese and any remaining breadcrumbs. Taste and adjust salt and pepper if necessary.

Pour into the prepared pan. Place the pan in a larger baking pan with 1–2 inches of near-boiling water. (You can put the pans in the oven and then pour the water in.)

Bake at 325° for 50–60 minutes or until the timbale is firm in the center and golden on top. Let rest a few minutes before removing from the pan.

Place whole on a serving platter with sauce over and/or under. Or slice before serving, put down the sauce first and the slices on top so the colors show.

Variations: The timbale can be made with just one vegetable, although the onion is a particularly zesty and flavorful ingredient to include in addition.

Other combinations of vegetables can be used: chard, potatoes, corn, peppers.

For a "Chawan Mushi" variation: Leave out the dairy products. Make the "custard" with eggs and the juices of the cooked vegetables and the cooking liquid. Omit the cheese. Season with soy sauce.

Prepare the vegetables as above and follow the same procedure for baking, although it probably will not slice well. It is usually baked (or steamed, actually) in small ceramic or ovenproof cups.

Chili Rellenos Souffle

This souffle is good served with a fresh, spicy salsa (the red sauce from the Tortilla Casserole on page 172, for instance). The recipe is simple. Of all of our souffle dishes, this one works time and time again. The souffle is aromatic with a reddish-golden hue. And the cheese-stuffed chilies hidden on the bottom make a delightful surprise.

Yields 4 servings
Preheat oven to 325°

For the chilies:
6 large fresh or canned poblano (green) chilies
1½–2 cups coarsely grated Jack, Cheddar, or mozzarella cheese

Roast the fresh chilies directly over a flame until the skin is completely charred. (The canned chilies are ready to be stuffed.)

Put them in a covered bowl (or jar with lid) to steam for 15 minutes, then remove the skin, rinse, and blot dry. (If you are using canned chilies, rinse them well in several changes of water, then dry.)

Pull out the seeds by removing the stem with a small knife and pulling the seed cluster free.

Stuff the chilies loosely with the cheese, then lay them side by side in a buttered 2-quart casserole.

For the souffle:
2 tablespoons butter
1 cup minced green onions, both green and white parts
¼ teaspoon salt
¼ teaspoon paprika
1 teaspoon chili powder
2 tablespoons flour
1 cup milk or light cream
¾ cup grated Jack, Cheddar, or mozzarella cheese
3 eggs, separated
2–3 tablespoons fresh herbs (parsley, cilantro, oregano)

Melt the butter in a saucepan and cook the green onions over a low heat until they are soft.

Add the salt, paprika, chili powder, and flour. Continue to cook over low heat for 5 minutes, stirring frequently.

Whisk in the milk gradually and continue to cook, stirring constantly, until the sauce thickens.

Remove the pan from the heat, then stir in the cheese.

Beat the egg yolks in a small bowl, and gradually whisk in a cup or so of the sauce to warm them. Then return the egg mixture to the sauce and stir until blended.

Taste and adjust with extra salt or chili powder if required.

Beat the egg whites until stiff. Then, fold them into the sauce along with the fresh herbs.

Pour the mixture over the chilies and bake at 325° until the souffle is puffed and nearly set, about 40 minutes.

Serve immediately.

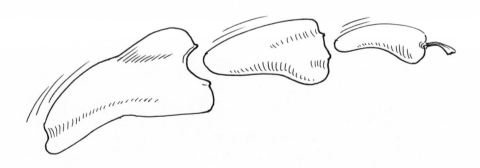

Mustard Butter Pasta with Broccoli

This has become our standard summertime pasta, with a flavor as bright as the colors. The pasta and vegetables cook together before being tossed in the mustard butter. The recipe is adaptable to a wide range of vegetables (see *Variations*).

⅝ cup butter (may be part olive or soy oil)
4 tablespoons Dijon mustard (or your favorite)
2 cloves garlic
2 tablespoons parsley, well minced
2 tablespoons chives, finely sliced, OR green onion, sliced and minced
salt & pepper
1 tablespoon oil
2 cups broccoli, cut into small flowerettes
¾ pound pasta, fettucine or linguine

Serves 4

Set out the butter early to soften up. When it's soft, blend in the mustard.

Slice the garlic and pound it in a mortar with a healthy pinch of salt. When it is fairly pulpy, add the parsley and chives (or green onion) and continue pounding for a short while to release their flavors.

Blend this mixture into the butter, along with a few twists of black pepper.

Use a large pot to boil a generous amount of water with a teaspoon of salt and a tablespoon of oil.

Fan the pasta into the boiling water. If you are using fresh pasta, add the broccoli at the same time. When using dried pasta, add the broccoli the last couple of minutes of cooking.

As soon as they are done, scoop out the pasta and the vegetables with an oval strainer, or drain in a colander. Put the pasta and broccoli in a 12-inch skillet, allowing some of the water to dribble in with it.

Add the prepared butter and, over moderate heat, toss the pasta with tongs until it is evenly coated. Keep the heat low enough that the butter does not bubble or fry—that will change the flavor.

Check the seasoning and add salt and pepper if necessary.

Variations: The simplest variation involves replacing some of the broccoli with small flowerettes of cauliflower. For additional color and flavor, use some carrot cut into matchsticks.

Another possibility is to use zucchini or crookneck squash, cherry tomatoes, peas, carrots. Cut the squash into 2-inch sections and then lengthwise into strips. Cut the carrots into matchsticks and the cherry tomatoes in half. Cook the squash, peas, and carrots with the pasta as in the basic recipe. Add the tomatoes with the mustard butter when tossing in the skillet.

Moussaka

This wonderfully aromatic, vegetarian interpretation of the traditional Greek eggplant gratin provides a bountiful dinner. Three parts are assembled in the final casserole: the eggplant, a tomato sauce, and a white sauce. It's worth the effort and nothing is complicated about the preparation.

Note: Start the navy beans for the tomato sauce in advance of the other preparations.

Yields 4–6 generous servings
Preheat oven to 425°

For the eggplant:
2 1–1¼-pound eggplants (2–2½ pound total)
olive oil
salt

Slice the eggplant ½ inch thick, layer it in a colander, and salt each layer. Press down the salted slices using a plate with a can of olive oil on it (or some other arrangement your kitchen provides). Let this sit until the bitter juices pebble the surface of the eggplant—about 30 minutes.

Rinse the eggplant and pat it dry.

Brush both sides with olive oil and bake in a 425° oven until browned. The bottoms will brown first, in 10–15 minutes. Turn the pieces over and bake another 10 minutes until the second side is done. Reduce the heat to 375°. Set aside the eggplant.

For the tomato sauce:
3 tablespoons olive oil
1 medium onion, chopped small
2 large cloves garlic, minced
½ teaspoon dried Greek oregano
½ teaspoon paprika
1 teaspoon cinnamon, freshly ground
good pinch ground clove
1 teaspoon salt
½ cup chopped fresh parsley

2 cups ripe tomatoes, peeled, seeded, and chopped (or canned tomatoes if good fresh ones aren't available)
¾ cup red wine
⅔ cup navy beans cooked in 1½ quarts water with a bay leaf, 3–4 sage leaves, and four cloves garlic (2–2½ hours, or pressure cook 12 minutes)

Heat the olive oil and cook the onions and garlic over a medium-low heat until the onions begin to soften.

Add the herbs and spices and continue to cook until the onions are completely soft. Then, raise the heat and add the tomatoes, wine, and cooked beans. Bring to a boil then lower the heat and cook slowly until the sauce is thick.

Taste and adjust the seasonings.

For the white sauce:
⅓ cup cream
1½ cups milk
1½ tablespoons butter
1½ tablespoons flour
2 egg yolks
⅓ pound ricotta cheese
1 cup grated Parmesan Reggiano
nutmeg, salt & white pepper

Combine the milk and cream and heat.

Melt the butter in a sauté pan, add the flour, and cook for 5 minutes.

Whisk in the warm milk-cream mixture.

Stir until the sauce is thickened and cook over low heat for 20 minutes, stirring occasionally.

Remove from the heat and whisk it slowly into the egg yolks. Add the ricotta and half the Parmesan cheese.

Season to taste with nutmeg, salt, and white pepper.

To assemble the Moussaka:

Cover the bottom of a 3-quart gratin dish with a shallow layer of the tomato/navy bean sauce. Over that, set half the eggplant, salt and pepper, and the reserved half-cup of Parmesan cheese. Distribute the remaining tomato sauce over the entire surface. Cover this with the remaining eggplant, salt, and pepper, then pour the white sauce over the top.

Bake in a preheated 375° oven for 40 minutes–1 hour, until the top is set and browned. Remove from the oven and allow to rest 20 minutes before serving.

Tortilla Casserole

I do not know if this is really a genuine Mexican recipe, but it is hot and colorful—and delightfully extravagant, not dollar-wise, but bounteous-feeling. A red sauce, a green sauce, beans, cheese, tortillas, and chilies assemble in a kind of Dagwood sandwich.

Both the beans and the red sauce call for roasted cumin seeds and roasted oregano, so you can roast them at the same time, but, note, the cumin gets started before adding the oregano.

Serrano chilies are fairly small and cylindrical (about 1½–2 inches long and ⅜ inch in diameter). The seeds are the hottest part, so be careful while handling (some people use rubber gloves). If you want *hot*, leave the seeds in.

For the beans:
½ cup black beans, OR ½ cup pinto beans
2 cups water
¼ teaspoon cumin seed, roasted and ground
¼ teaspoon oregano, roasted
½ teaspoon paprika
salt to taste
¼ teaspoon canned chilpotle peppers, finely minced, OR garlic and red
*   pepper*

Serves 4–6

Sort through the beans and remove any small stones or foreign matter. Rinse them off and cook with 2 cups water for 2 hours, or pressure cook at 15 pounds pressure for 20 minutes.

Drain and reserve excess water. Partially mash the beans, adding the reserved water as needed to make the beans creamy.

Salt to taste and add the seasonings. Although there is no real substitute for chilpotle peppers, you can try some garlic or red pepper to make the beans spicier.

For the red sauce:
1 medium yellow onion, sliced
2 cloves garlic, minced
oil for sautéing
1 or 2 serrano chilies, de-seeded, coarsely minced, OR *red pepper* OR
  cayenne (to taste)
2½ cups tomatoes, quartered
½ teaspoon cumin seed, roasted and ground
½ teaspoon oregano, roasted and powdered
salt & pepper

Sauté the onions and garlic in the oil for a few minutes. Add the chilies
and continue frying for a couple of minutes.

Add the tomatoes and seasonings.

Simmer for 15–20 minutes. If you want a smoother sauce, it can be
sieved or blended.

For the green sauce:
1½ cups tomatillos
1 medium red onion, sliced
1 clove garlic, coarsely minced
1 serrano chili, de-seeded, coarsely minced
4–5 sprigs cilantro leaves, minced
⅓ cup water (cooking liquid from the tomatillos)
salt

Remove the husks from the tomatillos and cover with water. Simmer
until soft but not mushy. Drain off and reserve the cooking liquid.

Sauté the onions and garlic for a few minutes, and then continue sautéing with the chilies.

Add the cooked tomatillos, the cilantro, cooking liquid (as needed), and
salt. Simmer for 15–20 minutes.

Blend or sieve for a smoother sauce.

(You can also buy a green taco sauce made with tomatillos if you cannot
get fresh tomatillos. It is also sometimes possible to buy "peeled green
tomatoes" which are already-cooked tomatillos.)

For assembling:
12 corn tortillas
corn oil
2 cups mild Cheddar, grated
1 cup Jack cheese, grated
½ cup Parmesan, grated
4-ounce can Ortega green chilies
1 cup sour cream or creme fraiche

Fry the tortillas in hot oil very briefly, 5–10 seconds a side. Drain on paper towels.

Preheat oven to 350°. Oil the casserole dish and assemble as follows (from the bottom up—starting with "4 tortillas"):

½ the Cheddar
½ the red sauce
½ the beans
4 tortillas
Jack and Parmesan cheese
all the green sauce
Ortega chilies
4 tortillas
½ the Cheddar
½ the red sauce
½ the beans
4 tortillas

Bake at 350° for about 30 minutes if the sauces are warm; longer, if they are cold. It does not need more cooking, just thorough heating.

Put the sour cream or *creme fraiche* on top at serving time.

Polenta & Mushroom Gratin

Polenta must be one of the most delicious ways of eating corn known. Add mushrooms and cheese and the corn is raised to even greater heights.

This is a four-part recipe, but the procedures are straightforward, the results gratifying. First, the polenta is cooked, and while it cools and sets, the mushrooms are sliced and cooked. Their liquid, if any, is reserved for the third part, the cream sauce. The fourth step is assembling the gratin; this can be done hours in advance of the final baking.

For the polenta:
1 tablespoon butter
4 cups boiling water with 1 teaspoon salt
1½ cups coarse cornmeal

Makes 4–6 servings

Melt the butter in the boiling water, then whisk in the cornmeal. Lower the heat and cook 25 minutes, stirring continually. The mixture will be very thick.

Pour the polenta into an ungreased breadpan, smooth the top, and then set aside to cool.

For the mushrooms:
2 tablespoons each butter and olive oil
1 pound mushrooms, sliced ¼-inch thick
½ ounce dried Italian, Japanese, or Chinese mushrooms, soaked and
  sliced (optional)
2 cloves garlic, minced
salt & freshly grated pepper
1½ teaspoons fresh thyme leaves, chopped OR *½ teaspoon dried thyme*

Heat the butter and olive oil in a skillet until hot. Add the mushrooms, toss to coat, then reduce the heat. If dried mushrooms—soaked and sliced—are being used, they can be added at this time.

Add the garlic, salt, pepper, and thyme. Cook until the mushrooms release their juices. Drain and reserve the juice, and set the mushrooms aside.

For the cream sauce:
2 tablespoons butter
2 tablespoons flour
mushroom juices, from above, plus enough milk or light cream to make
  2 cups
salt & freshly grated pepper
nutmeg, freshly ground

Melt the butter in a saucepan over low heat. Add the flour and cook for about 3–4 minutes. Whisk in the liquid and continue to cook, stirring, until the sauce thickens.

Season with salt, pepper, and nutmeg. Cook over low heat for 10 minutes, stirring. Be moderate with the amount of nutmeg; the flavor can be overwhelming.

Assembling the casserole:
½ cup Parmesan cheese, freshly grated
1 cup fontina cheese (or Monterey Jack or Swiss), grated
fresh herbs, to garnish

Preheat oven to 350°. Lightly oil a baking dish (8-inch baking dish for a 2-layer gratin or a large, flat baking dish for a single layer gratin).

Turn out the polenta and slice it into pieces ½–¾-inch thick.

Pour a little cream sauce in the bottom of the baking dish and arrange half the polenta slices on top. Over this distribute half the mushrooms, half the Parmesan and fontina cheese, a good grinding of pepper and half the remaining sauce.

Layer in the rest of the polenta and the remaining ingredients in the same order, ending with the sauce.

Cover and bake for 30 minutes, or until the gratin is bubbling hot. It will take longer if the ingredients have all cooled. Remove the lid and bake another 5 minutes.

Serve with a fresh green garnish: minced parsley, chervil, or a scattering of marjoram and thyme leaves.

Polenta Eggplant Gratin

I have always found this dish exciting and stimulating, especially with a good Pinot Noir. The polenta provides a welcome earthiness in contrast to the herbaceous qualities of the eggplant and tomato sauce and the richness of the cheese. There are several parts to the recipe, but nothing very mysterious or complex. It takes a while, but it is time giving life, time well offered.

For the polenta:
1 cup coarse corn meal (polenta)
3 cups water
pinch of salt
⅓ cup grated cheese (fontina, Jack, Swiss, or what-have-you)
⅙ cup smoked cheese, grated (or more of above)
1–2 tablespoons butter

Serves 4–6

Whisk the corn meal into 3 cups boiling salted water. Simmer over moderately low heat for 30 minutes. Use a thick-bottomed pot, if you have one, or stir often to prevent scorching.

Stir in the grated cheeses and butter. (This is a good use for pieces of dried cheese that are no longer good for eating fresh. Some smoked cheese adds a marvelous touch here, but it is too strong to use straight.)

Pour out into pans about 1-inch thick and cool completely.

For the tomato sauce:
1 medium red onion, diced
olive oil for frying
2 cloves of garlic, pressed or minced
½ cup red wine
2 1-pound tins of canned tomatoes, drained and chunked
salt & pepper
2 tablespoons fresh basil, minced

Sauté the onions in the olive oil until soft. Add the garlic and continue cooking a couple minutes.

Add the red wine and stew a few minutes while stirring.

Add the tomatoes and simmer for a good while: 40 minutes to an hour or more.

Season with salt and pepper. Stir in the chopped basil.

For the eggplant:
1 eggplant, cut into fork-size chunks, OR 4 Japanese eggplants, cut into
    ¾-inch thick slices
olive oil
salt
oregano, dried or fresh

Brush the eggplant slices with olive oil, sprinkle with salt and oregano. Bake at 350° until soft, about 45–50 minutes. Turn the slices over after about 25 minutes.

For assembling the gratin:
1 cup fontina cheese (or Jack or Swiss), grated
½ cup Parmesan cheese (or asiago or Romano), grated

Cut the cooled polenta into chunks. They can be whatever size you want.

Assemble the ingredients in a large casserole in layers: sauce, polenta, eggplant, cheese, sauce, polenta, eggplant, sauce, cheese; or a more simple arrangement: sauce, polenta, cheese, eggplant, sauce, cheese.

Bake covered at 350° until everything is hot, about 45 minutes. Uncover the last 5 minutes to brown the top slightly.

Desserts

Once there were two friends who became monks, joining a monastery together. Both were devoted to their religious practice, yet both still enjoyed smoking now and again. The monastic routine was rigorous, but they found idle moments during the day to relax with a cigarette.

When the two first entered the monastery, they had thought that they would soon give up smoking, but instead they discovered it a rare pleasure to light up, puff on their cigarettes, watch the smoke curl and drift, and chat about the affairs of the day. And so, even after a couple years of monastic practice, they found their love for smoking had waxed rather than waned.

One day, while they sat smoking, they talked it over, saying to each other that they really ought to find some way to integrate their religious life with their smoking. "We've been here quite a while, and since we do not want to give up smoking, we must find some way to make it part of our religious life," they thought.

So, shortly after this, one of them went to speak with the Abbot, saying, "I've been here a couple years, and this practice has been very beneficial for me, and I am devoted to prayer. But there is one thing which I have not been able to give up. I still enjoy smoking, and I want all my activities to be part of my religious life, so I was wondering if it would be all right for me to smoke during prayer."

The Abbot was aghast. "Absolutely not," he responded. "Prayer is just for praying. You must never bring in any other activities."

Crestfallen, the monk returned to his friend and reported that the Abbot was completely unsympathetic, that he did not seem to have any comprehension of what they were trying to do, and that it would be useless to speak with him further on the subject. Undaunted, the second monk said he would give it a try.

So the second monk soon went to see the Abbot and said, as the first monk had said, that he really was grateful to be able to participate in the religious life of the monastery, but the fact was, that in spite of himself, he still enjoyed smoking. "And I was wondering," he asked, "if it would be all right if I was to pray while I smoked."

"By all means," replied the Abbot, "Whatever you are doing, you should also be praying."

Desserts

During the hot Tassajara summer, sorbets, ices, and ice creams are very popular desserts. However, we have a limited amount of electricity, no freezer, and a great demand for whatever ice the ice machine produces. Having frozen desserts means no ice for cold drinks in the afternoon, so there is always a tradeoff: a sign goes up on the ice machine warning away would-be ice takers.

With the frozen desserts, we sometimes have fresh fruits or cookies. Other evenings we most often serve one of our cakes.

At lunch, we used to make dozens of cookies, but lately we have found an assortment of dried fruits, fresh fruits, and nuts to be quite satisfying. The cookies go in bag lunches for a day's outing.

Sour Cream Poppyseed Cake

A tender, moist cake that is one of the all-time favorites (year-in, year-out) at the Tassajara Bread Bakery in San Francisco. Serve plain, dusted with powdered sugar, or frosted with cream cheese icing. It's also good with ripe, red strawberries and whipped cream or vanilla *crème anglaise* (page 208).

½ cup butter
¾–1 cup sugar
3 egg yolks
1 teaspoon vanilla
1 cup all-purpose flour or cake flour, sifted before measuring
½ teaspoon salt
½ teaspoon baking soda
½ cup sour cream
3 egg whites
⅓ cup poppy seeds

Yields 1 8-inch loaf
Preheat oven to 350°

Butter and flour an 8-inch tube pan.

Cream the butter and sugar until fluffy, beat in the egg yolks one at a time, and add the vanilla.

Sift the flour, salt, and baking soda together and fold them into the butter mixture alternately with the sour cream.

Beat the egg whites until they form stiff peaks, then fold into the batter.

Fold in the poppy seeds, then pour the batter into the prepared pan.

Bake in the center of a preheated 350° oven until the top is brown and firm to the touch and a toothpick comes out clean when inserted in the center, about 45 minutes.

Mom's Mexican Chocolate Cake

This is from Eric Larson's mom, and she's on to a good thing: a moist chocolate cake flavored with cinnamon, almonds, and coffee. Serve with a softly whipped cream—almond, vanilla, or kahlua flavored—or with buttery Mocha Icing (recipe follows cake instructions). If you are *really* into chocolate, a little chocolate-chocolate chip ice cream on the side is certainly called for. In that case, however, don't let anyone but your closest friends know about your indulgence—and be sure they join in with you.

½ cup butter
1 cup sugar
3 eggs
1½ tablespoons vanilla
⅛ teaspoon almond extract
2 cups unbleached white flour
½ teaspoon salt
2 teaspoons cinnamon,

preferably freshly ground in a spice mill
1 teaspoon baking powder
¼ teaspoon baking soda
½ cup buttermilk
4 ounces semisweet chocolate
¾ cup water
2 tablespoons instant coffee

Makes 2 8-inch layers
Preheat oven to 350°

Butter and flour 2 8-inch cake pans.

Cream the butter and sugar until light. Beat in the eggs one at a time, then add the vanilla and almond extracts.

Sift the dry ingredients together and fold them into the butter mixture, alternating with the buttermilk.

In a small saucepan, combine the chocolate, water, and coffee over low heat, stirring until smooth and melted.

Add the chocolate mixture to the batter and stir to blend. Then pour into the prepared cake pans.

Bake in the center of the preheated 350° oven until the cakes are firm on top and pull away from the sides of the pans, about 45 minutes.

Rotate the pans from front to back in the oven midway through the baking so they cook evenly.

Turn out on cake racks to cool.

MOCHA ICING

6 ounces semisweet chocolate
½ cup strong coffee
1 teaspoon vanilla
6 ounces (1½ sticks) butter

Yields enough to ice the tops
and sides of 2 8-inch cakes

Put the chocolate, coffee, and vanilla in a small, heavy saucepan and set over a medium-low heat. Stir frequently to avoid burning.

When melted, pour into a bowl and beat in the butter. As the frosting cools it will thicken to spreading consistency.

Spread on the top and sides of the cake.

Give the whole cake away to a friend, and know the joy of chocolate generosity. Perhaps a piece of it will come back.

Lemon Pudding Cake

Fragrant and light on the palate, this cake possesses a tart refreshing flavor. The combination of pudding and cake is appealing and enjoyable, the best of two worlds in one.

3 tablespoons butter
1 cup sugar
grated peel of 4 lemons
5 egg yolks
6 tablespoons all-purpose flour
5 tablespoons lemon juice
1½ cups milk or light cream
5 egg whites
⅛ teaspoon salt

Makes 6 servings
Preheat oven to 350°

Cream the butter, sugar, and grated lemon peels together. Then add the yolks, one at a time, beating well after each addition.

When all the yolks are incorporated and the mixture is smooth and light, stir in the flour, alternating with the milk and lemon juice.

Beat the egg whites and salt until stiff peaks are formed and fold into the batter.

Bake at 350° in an 8-inch baking dish or individual cups set in a water bath for 45 minutes, or until the top is golden brown and set.

Serve with sweetened whipped cream if desired.

Orange Raisin Walnut Cake

Scented, fruited, nutty, this cake is reminiscent of carrot cake (without the carrots). The orange syrup provides an unusual moistness and an appealing fragrance, especially if you add the final optional ingredients, and saves having to think about frosting or icing.

1 cup raisins, plumped in hot
 water
½ cup walnuts
zest of one large orange
½ cup butter
¾ cup sugar or brown sugar
1 teaspoon vanilla
2 large eggs
2½ cups flour

1 teaspoon baking soda
1 teaspoon salt
1 cup buttermilk
juice of one large orange
4 tablespoons honey
orange flower water
rum, Curaçao, or Grand Marnier
 (optional)

Makes a 1-layer 8-inch cake
Preheat oven to 300°

Butter and flour an 8-inch cake pan and line the bottom with parchment paper or foil.

Cover the raisins with hot water and then drain them. With the walnuts and orange zest (which can be removed in strips with a vegetable peeler), grind the raisins in a food mill or blender to make a coarse purée that retains some texture. (It may be necessary to use a little of the juice if the mixture is too dry.)

Cream the butter and sugar together until they are light. Add the vanilla and beat in the eggs, one at a time.

Combine and sift the flour, soda, and salt.

Alternating with the buttermilk, blend the dry ingredients into the butter/sugar mixture, until all are incorporated. You will have a smooth, thick batter.

Fold in the raisin-walnut mixture and then pour the batter into the pan.

Tap once or twice on the counter to settle the batter then bake at 300° from 50 minutes to an hour, or until the cake is firm to the touch.

When the cake is done, remove it from the pan and peel off the baking parchment.

Reverse the cake and let it cool while you make a syrup of the orange juice and honey. Boil the two together and flavor with a little orange flower water, if you have it.

Brush all the syrup over the top of the cake. It will sink into the cake and make it very moist.

Of course, if you'd like to soak the cake with a little rum, that's fine. Also, Curaçao or Grand Marnier—if you keep such things around. Pour on a shot or two. Give the cake a swig.

Use care when transferring the cooled cake to a cake plate—perhaps a few wide spatulas would help.

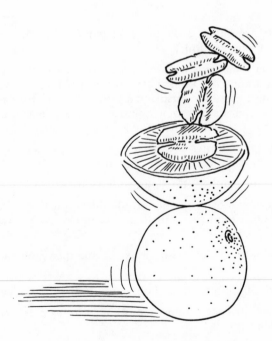

Fresh Ginger Gingerbread

With its marvelous blend of spices, this well-spiced cake makes a great dessert that can finish off a dull, drab dinner with a kick. And if you don't know how to make a dull, drab dinner, you can serve the gingerbread to finish off an exciting, seasonal dinner with a flourish. You can't go wrong!

Dry ingredients
¾ cup white pastry flour or all-purpose flour
¾ cup whole wheat pastry flour
1 teaspoon baking powder
¾ teaspoon freshly ground cinnamon
¼ teaspoon grated nutmeg
¼ teaspoon ground cloves
¼ teaspoon salt
¼ teaspoon mustard powder
pinch of cayenne
pinch of black pepper

Wet ingredients:
¼ cup butter
¼ cup brown sugar
3 tablespoons fresh ginger root, peeled and grated finely
½ cup molasses
½ teaspoon baking soda
¾ cup boiling water
¼ teaspoon baking soda
2 eggs, beaten

Makes 1 8-inch cake
Preheat oven to 350°

Sift all the dry ingredients together.

Cream the butter and sugar together and add the ginger.

Beat the molasses and the ½ teaspoon baking soda together until the color lightens and little bubbles form.

Combine the boiling water and the ¼ teaspoon baking soda.

Add the butter-ginger-sugar mixture to the molasses and mix thoroughly.

Add the dry ingredients alternately with the boiling water-soda, beginning and ending with the dry ingredients.

When this is finished, fold in the beaten eggs.

Pour the batter into a thoroughly buttered and floured cake pan and bake at 350° for 30 minutes, or until a toothpick comes out clean.

Serve with piles of softly whipped cream, or gobs of vanilla ice cream.

Dried Fruit & Nut Spice Cake

This is an "allergy invention," which became a standard dessert. It does call for eggs and a little cornstarch, but no flour, sweetener, or dairy products. Plenty sweet, rich, and moist, it needs no topping, but you can top it with a glaze or whipped cream if you want.

Note: you can use any combination of dried fruits.

¾ cup apple juice
½ cup pitted prunes, chopped
¾ cup raisins and/or currants
1 cup pitted dates, chopped
2 tablespoons soy oil (or other "flavorless" oil)
2 packed cups walnut or pecan "flour" (see instructions)
¼ cup potato starch or corn-starch

1 teaspoon baking powder
½ teaspoon baking soda
¼ teaspoon ground cloves
½ teaspoon ground nutmeg
¼ teaspoon allspice
1½ teaspoon cinnamon
½ teaspoon salt
5 eggs

Makes 1 8–9-inch round cake
Preheat oven to 275°

Heat the apple juice almost to boiling and pour it over the prunes and raisins.

Mash the chopped dates thoroughly, blending in the oil.

Grind very finely enough pecans or walnuts to make 2 packed cups. This is the "flour," so make it as fine as you can, using a hand mill, blender, or Cuisinart.

Sift the potato or corn starch with the baking powder, baking soda, spices, and salt. Combine with the ground nuts.

Separate the eggs. Beat the yolks, one at a time, into the date-oil mixture.

Blend in the nut mixture and the dried fruit-apple juice mixture.

Beat the egg whites until stiff but not dry. Fold half into the batter, a little at a time. Then gently fold in the rest.

Grease and flour the cake pan, pour in the batter, and bake at 275° until a toothpick inserted in the center comes out clean.

190

Bibi's Apple Kuchen

This recipe came to us from Austria, courtesy of Emila, who got the recipe from Bibi, a former Playmate-of-the-Month from Sweden. Where the recipe originates remains unclear, but, wherever it started, the dessert is mouth-watering: the pastry, sweet and buttery; the apples, sweet/tart and spicy.

Dough:
2 cups unbleached pastry flour or all-purpose flour
½ cup sugar
1 teaspoon baking powder
¼ teaspoon salt
¾ cup plus 2 tablespoons butter, at room temperature
1 egg yolk
1 teaspoon vanilla extract

Filling:
3 cups apples, thinly sliced
juice and grated peel of one lemon
2 tablespoons sugar
2 teaspoons cinnamon
⅓ cup raisins

Makes 1 pastry that will serve 4–6 people

Sift together the dry dough ingredients. Work in the butter with your fingers until you have a crumbly dough.

Add the egg yolk and the vanilla and continue to work the dough. It will crumble and look like pie dough, but keep working with it until it becomes somewhat soft and pliable.

Shape the dough into a flat disk, wrap it in waxed paper or plastic wrap, and set it in the refrigerator for a half hour.

Toss the apple slices with the lemon juice and peel, the sugar, cinnamon, and raisins.

Remove the dough from the refrigerator and work it a little to soften it up. Then roll it out on a piece of waxed paper or a clean dish towel (about 14 inches long and 8 inches wide).

Place the apples lengthwise along one edge and then use the waxed paper (or towel) to help roll the dough over the apples and into a log shape and seal the ends. Lifting it with the waxed paper, transfer the log to a baking sheet.

Brush the dough with a little sweetened cream or melted butter (or the leftover beaten egg white).

Bake the pastry at 325° until the crust is light golden brown, about 40 minutes. Overbaking will make it dry.

Serve warm, dusted with powdered sugar, and accompanied with softly whipped cream flavored with cognac.

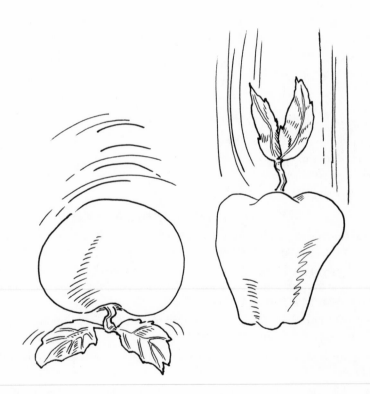

Apple Walnut Sour Cream Bread

This is a tender, golden brown loaf, best made in the fall when new crop apples and fresh walnuts are at their peak. Known as a dessert bread, this could also be served with a special holiday dinner.

½ cup butter, plus extra butter for the pan
½ cup brown sugar
2 eggs
1 teaspoon vanilla
1 cup all-purpose flour
1 teaspoon ground cardamon
1 teaspoon baking soda
1 teaspoon baking powder
½ teaspoon salt
1 cup sour cream
2 cups chopped apples
½–1 cup chopped walnuts

Makes 1 9-inch loaf
Preheat oven to 350°

Butter and flour a 9-inch bread pan.

Cream the butter and sugar until fluffy.

Add the eggs and vanilla and beat until smooth.

Sift the dry ingredients together and, alternating with the sour cream, gently fold them into the butter-egg mixture. The batter will be very thick, but avoid overworking it.

Fold in the apples and walnuts.

Spread the batter into the prepared pan and smooth the top.

Bake in a preheated 350° oven for 1 hour, or until the top is firm to the touch and a deep golden brown.

Allow the bread to cool at least 10 minutes before slicing.

Serve with cream cheese or a buttery cheese like St. André or Brie.

Fig Bread

This sweet, rather cake-like bread is one of our regular luncheon desserts or tea snacks. We leave the figs whole, to appear as tasty slabs once the bread is sliced, but they could be sliced into rounds.

1 cup apple or orange juice
1½ cups mission figs, de-stemmed but left whole
¼ teaspoon salt
¼ cup butter
2 eggs
⅓ cup sugar
½ teaspoon vanilla
1 teaspoon lemon or orange rind, grated
1¾ cups pastry flour
½ teaspoon baking powder
¼ teaspoon baking soda

Makes 1 medium loaf
Preheat oven to 350°

Heat the juice almost to boiling and pour it over the figs, salt, and butter in a mixing bowl. Stir to melt the butter and set aside in the refrigerator to cool.

Beat the eggs, then beat in the sugar, vanilla, and fruit rind. Stir this into the well-cooled (room temperature) fig mixture.

Sift the flour together with the baking powder and baking soda. Mix into the wet ingredients with a minimum number of strokes.

Grease and flour a medium-sized loaf pan, pour in the batter, and bake at 350° for about an hour, until a toothpick comes out clean.

Coffee Almond Butter Cookies

The coffee flavor comes as a surprise in what is already an excellent almond butter cookie.

1 cup unsalted butter
¾ cup brown sugar
4½ teaspoons instant coffee
½ teaspoon salt
¼ teaspoon almond extract
1 cup finely chopped almonds
½ cup semisweet chocolate (optional), *cut into various-sized pieces smaller than the intended size of the cookies*
2 cups all-purpose flour

Yields 2½ dozen cookies
Preheat oven to 350°

Cream the butter and sugar together, then mix in the coffee, salt, and almond extract.

Fold in the almonds, chocolate (optional), and then mix in the flour.

Roll the dough into inch-size balls. Flatten with a glass or the heel of your palm.

Bake at 350° for 15 minutes or until they are lightly browned.

Oatmeal Shortbread

With a delicate caramel flavor and a substantial texture worthy of lingering over, this shortbread proves easy to make—and not so difficult to eat either.

½ cup butter, at room temperature
⅔ cup brown sugar
⅔ cup rolled oats
¾ cup plus 2 tablespoons all-purpose flour

Makes 1 9-inch round
Preheat oven to 300°

Put all the ingredients in a bowl and work them together with your fingers until you have a soft, uniform dough.

Press the dough into a 9-inch pie pan, mark the edges with the tines of a fork, and score deeply so that it will be easy to cut into pieces.

Bake in the 300° preheated oven for 25–30 minutes until firm and only lightly browned. Be careful not to overbake or the shortbread will be hard.

Following the score lines, slice the shortbread into wedges while still warm.

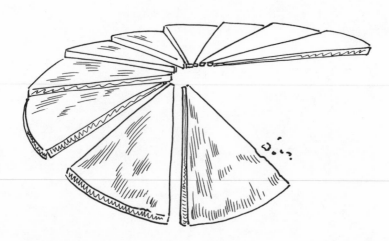

Pecan Dreams

This is a recipe from Brian's sister's friend's mom, and who knows where before that. This is the way cookies were meant to be before we worried about butter, sugar, white flour, salt, and whether or not the nuts were rancid. If you can get by that without drinking the rum and vanilla extracts, you've got yourself a cookie; otherwise, just dreams.

1 cup butter
½ cup sifted powdered sugar
2 teaspoons vanilla
2 teaspoons water or rum
½ teaspoon salt
2 cups sifted all-purpose flour
2 cups pecans, finely chopped
sifted powdered sugar to garnish

Yields 3 dozen 1-inch cookies
Preheat oven to 325°

Cream the butter and powdered sugar until fluffy, then beat in the vanilla, water or rum, and salt.

Stir the flour into the butter mixture, then add the pecans, and stir to make an evenly textured dough.

Roll the dough into 1¼ inch balls and place on an unbuttered cookie sheet.

Bake in the upper third of the 325° oven for 20 minutes.

Remove the cookies to a cooling rack to firm.

While still warm, roll the cookies in the powdered sugar.

Remember, "no sugar, no enlightenment,"—don't let the cookies sit around too long.

Variations: Use walnuts or almonds in place of the pecans.

Brian's Chocolate Chip Cookies

You've had Toll House, Famous Amos, and Mrs. Fields. And among all these, you probably have your favorite. Here is ours (for now). Three things distinguish this cookie: a touch of molasses, some instant coffee, and chocolate cut to bits. (The kitchen staff at our farm, Green Gulch, is going through a whole book of chocolate chip cookie recipes and compiling rankings, but Brian's cookies have yet to be rated.) The chocolate pieces can range in size from powder and crumbs to pieces as large as a shelled almond (anything smaller than the intended size of the cookie). If you use pre-formed chocolate chips, the cookie will not be the same.

1 cup butter, softened (room
   temperature)
⅔ cup brown sugar
2 eggs
2 teaspoons vanilla
2 teaspoons molasses
1 teaspoon instant coffee, finely
   powdered
1 cup white flour, unbleached

1 cup whole wheat pastry flour,
   or additional white flour
1 teaspoon baking soda
½ teaspoon salt
2 cups walnuts, finely chopped
14 ounces semisweet or
   bittersweet chocolate, chopped
   or cut into pieces with a knife

Makes 4 dozen cookies
Preheat oven to 375°

Cream the butter until free of lumps, then add the sugar, and cream until fluffy.

Add the eggs, one at a time, the vanilla, molasses, and coffee. Beat well.

Sift the dry ingredients together and mix them in.

Fold in the walnuts and chocolate pieces.

Form into balls one inch in diameter, place on a buttered and floured cookie sheet. Flatten slightly, then bake at 375° for 12 minutes, or until lightly browned underneath.

Glazed Cream Cheese Lemon Cookies

These lemony delights are a good cookie to serve with tea or with a fruit dessert such as Gingered Figs.

¾ *cup butter*
⅓ *cup cream cheese*
¾ *cup sugar*
1 egg
1 tablespoon grated lemon peel
1 tablespoon lemon juice
1 teaspoon baking powder
½ *teaspoon salt*
2 cups all-purpose flour
Lemon Glaze and finely chopped walnuts or almonds to garnish

Yields 3 dozen 1-inch cookies
Preheat oven to 375°

Cream the butter, cream cheese, and sugar until fluffy, then beat in the egg, lemon peel, and lemon juice.

Sift the dry ingredients together and gently mix them into the butter mixture.

Refrigerate the dough for at least 1 hour—this makes shaping the cookies easier.

Roll the dough into balls about 1 inch in diameter and place them on an unbuttered cookie sheet. (For a nicely rounded cookie, leave the dough in balls; for a thinner cookie, flatten the dough with the bottom of a glass dipped in sugar.)

Bake in the upper third of the 375° preheated oven for 12–15 minutes, or until the bottoms and edges of the cookies are light brown.

Transfer the cookies to a rack, let cool briefly, then dip in the Lemon Glaze and dust with finely chopped walnuts or almonds.

LEMON GLAZE

3–4 tablespoons lemon juice
1 cup sifted powdered sugar
½ cup finely chopped walnuts or almonds

Stir the lemon juice into the powdered sugar—it should have the consistency of thick cream. Put the glaze in a shallow dish to make it easy to dip the cookies. Sprinkle the nuts over the top while the glaze is still soft.

The nuts don't have to be set in place before the kids can try one—especially if they've been helping.

Date & Pecan Confection

Here is a rich, moist, cookie-like confection that Brian dreamed up. Great for people with allergies to wheat, butter, or eggs, and great for those without allergies too, this sweet tastes delicious to any tongue.

Note: If you don't have orange flower water, add ½ teaspoon of either orange peel or lemon peel, or omit.

1 cup pitted moist dates
2 cups pecans, finely ground
1 teaspoon orange flower water (from the liquor department)
30 pecan halves
powdered sugar (optional)

Yields 30 1½-inch cookies
Preheat oven to 325°

Roughly chop the dates. Then, using the back of a wooden spoon or your fingers, mix the dates with the ground pecans and the orange flower water until a dough is formed.

Roll the lumps of dough between your palms into walnut-size balls, place on an unbuttered baking sheet, then press a pecan into the center of each. (These cookies will not spread when baking so they can be placed close together.)

Bake in the upper third of the 325° preheated oven for 12–15 minutes or until the bottoms are lightly browned.

Serve plain or dusted with powdered sugar.

Sorbets

Sorbets—fresh fruit ices made without milk or cream—are marvelously refreshing, and pleasing on the palate. They are easy to make, especially if you have an ice cream freezer, and the combinations are endless. Use fruit that is quite ripe—it has the fullest, juiciest flavor. The pure fruit flavor will simply melt away in your mouth.

Here's the general formula:

4 cups fruit purée
1 cup sugar
citrus juice: lemon or lime
liquor: rum, brandy, Grand Marnier

To make the fruit purée, wash and pit the fruit, cut it into smallish pieces, and blend until smooth. (One former guest cook says, "I generally do not remove the skins from peaches and nectarines as I like the small flecks of color and texture they add to the finished product.")

Heat the fruit purée with the sugar until the sugar crystals dissolve. You may use less sugar if the fruit is very sweet, but remember that the frozen sorbet will taste somewhat less sweet than the unfrozen mixture.

Freeze in an ice cream freezer.

Add 1–2 tablespoons of lemon or lime juice to adjust sweetness/tartness. You will notice this freshens and enlivens the taste.

Add liquor to accent the flavor.

Store covered in the freezer compartment of your refrigerator.

Some suggested combinations: Peach and/or nectarine with lemon juice and rum, peach brandy, or Grand Marnier; strawberry with Kirsch; kiwi with lemon juice; melon with lime or lemon juice.

Tangerine Ice

Based on a recipe from Marcella Hazan, this ice uses orange, tangerine, and lemon juice to make a tangy cool dessert.

¾ cup sugar
2 cups freshly squeezed tangerine juice
1 cup freshly squeezed orange juice
½ cup freshly squeezed lemon juice
grated peel of 1 orange
grated peel of 1 lemon
3 tablespoons (or to taste) rum or Grand Marnier

Serves 4–6

Make a syrup of the sugar and enough of the fruit juice to melt the sugar crystals.

Mix the syrup with the rest of the juices and the grated peels.

Freeze either in an ice cream freezer or in ice cube trays.

When nearly frozen, add the liquor to taste, stirring to mix.

Return to freezer for at least an hour. If any of the liquor has separated, stir the ice again before serving.

Lime Milk Sherbet

This recipe is loosely based on a Fanny Farmer recipe.

1½ cups sugar
1 cup freshly squeezed lime juice
4 cups milk
1 tablespoon grated lime peel

Serves 4–6

Heat the sugar with some of the lime juice until the sugar crystals dissolve.

Mix this syrup together with the remaining lime juice, milk, and lemon peel.

Freeze in an ice cream freezer or in ice cube tray.

This will not, alas, be green, only lime-flavored.

The mixture may look curdled, unfrozen, but after freezing, it will be smooth, so don't worry.

Brian's Mango Ice Cream

Here is Brian's answer to the same-old-dessert syndrome.

3 cups mango pulp
¼ cup sugar or more to taste
1 cup whipping cream
1 tablespoon lime juice or more to taste

Serves 4

Put the mango pulp through a sieve to remove the fibers. Blend it with the sugar until liquefied.

Whip the cream until slightly thickened and mix thoroughly with the mango purée.

Add the lime juice to taste.

Freeze the mixture in an ice cream freezer.

Place the ice cream in a tightly covered container. Put in the freezer and allow to freeze hard.

Strawberry variation: Substitute strawberries for mango. Excellent!

Grapefruit Champagne Ice

A refreshing, non-filling dessert, this palate-cleansing, taste-titillating ice is especially appetizing in hot weather. The idea for this probably came from Richard Olney.

⅔ cup sugar
½ cup fresh orange juice
2 cups fresh grapefruit juice
1 cup champagne
¼ cup cognac

Serves 4

Heat the sugar with a bit of the fruit juices until the syrup is completely without crystals.

Mix the syrup together with the rest of the juices and the champagne. Taste for balance of flavors.

Freeze either in an ice cream maker or in an ice cube tray, stirring from time to time.

Once frozen, add the cognac, stirring in a bit at a time, tasting.

Return the ice to the freezer for at least 1 hour. Serve either in chilled bowls or in orange or grapefruit halves which have been scooped clean and either frozen or thoroughly chilled.

Lime Cream & Strawberries

Don't look for the cream to be green. You have to add food coloring for that. Still, the deep red of the berries and the off white of the cream are an elegant combination, and the flavors offer a delightful interplay of sweet, tart, and butterfat. What could be better?

3 egg yolks

5 tablespoons sugar

1 cup half-and-half (or cream)

peel of 1 small lime, zested or
   finely minced

1 pint strawberries

2 tablespoons sugar

juice of 2–3 limes

½ cup whipping cream

Serves 4

Beat the yolks and the 5 tablespoons of sugar together until light and lemon-colored.

Heat the half-and-half with the lime peel. Gradually whisk the heated cream into the yolks to warm them. Then, return this "custard" to the fire and cook gently—all the while continuing to whisk—until it coats the back of a spoon. Do not boil. It will still be liquid, but thickened slightly. (If it goes too far and "scrambles," toss the mixture in the Cuisinart.)

Strain out the peel and chill.

Rinse the berries and either dry them on toweling or let them drain for a while in a colander. Remove the stems (the end of a vegetable peeler is good for this). Slice them if they are large or leave them whole if they are small.

Sprinkle the berries with the sugar and toss them with the lime juice. Refrigerate.

Before serving, whip the cream so that it soft peaks. Fold it into the custard.

Divide the berries into serving dishes and spoon the lime cream over them. Or, put the lime cream in dishes and divide the berries over the dishes.

Contemplate your good fortune to be enjoying berries and lime cream.

Let your compassion know no bounds.

Vanilla Crème Anglaise

A classic custard cream for fresh fruit, simple cakes, or poached meringues, Vanilla Crème Anglaise can be either poured on top or served underneath the dessert in a pretty pool.

5 egg yolks
¼ cup sugar
2 cups light cream or milk
1 vanilla bean, split lengthwise OR *1 teaspoon vanilla extract*

Makes about 2½ cups

In a large bowl, beat the yolks and sugar until pale yellow and fluffy.

Combine the cream or milk and vanilla in a saucepan and heat to simmering. Then gradually whisk the milk mixture into the bowl with the egg mixture.

Return the hot liquid to the saucepan. Then cook over low heat, stirring constantly with a wooden spatula until the custard is thick enough to coat the back of the spatula (180° on an instant reading thermometer). While heating the custard, do not let it boil.

Immediately pour the custard into a bowl.

Scrape the little seeds out of the vanilla bean and add the pods to the custard.

Allow to cool completely, then strain through a fine sieve.

Persimmon Cream

This is a sensual, simple dessert. Serve it chilled, with a crisp walnut cookie (a variation of Pecan Dreams, see page 197). Use the large American persimmons, not the smaller Japanese persimmons which can be eaten while still crisp. The persimmons should be deep orange with black splotches and so soft they practically fall out of their skins. Estimate ½ cup persimmon purée per person.

ripe, soft persimmons
powdered sugar or honey
heavy cream
Marsala (optional)

Remove the skin from the persimmons and whisk the pulp lightly to break it up, leaving some texture.

Add powdered sugar or honey as needed to bring up the flavor of the fruit.

Using 1 part cream for every 4 parts persimmon, estimate the amount required and whisk the cream briskly until stiff.

Flavor the cream with Marsala if you wish, then fold it into the persimmon. Do not blend it completely; leave streaks of cream throughout.

Mound into dessert bowls and chill. Serve with 1 or 2 walnut cookies.

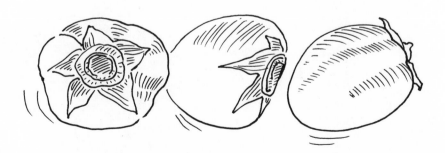

Gingered Figs

An intense fruit dessert, Gingered Figs are served often in the cold months before the fresh fruit arrives.

½ pound dried Mission figs
1 ounce peeled fresh ginger, thinly sliced (this is about two thumbs'
  worth)
2 cups water
½ cup honey
sour cream and grated lemon peel, to garnish

Serves 4

Discard the knobby stems of the figs.

Rinse and put the figs in a saucepan with the ginger, water, and honey.

Bring to a boil, then simmer over low heat until the figs are soft and the liquid has thickened to a dark syrup, about 25 minutes.

Chill and serve very cold with the sour cream flavored with a bit of grated lemon peel.

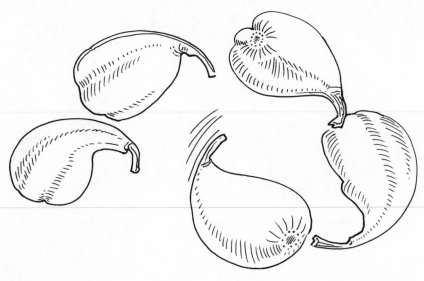

WASHING THIS POT

Washing this pot,
metal returns to metal,
flowers brilliant and shining.
In heart work
arms, fingers, toes,
feelings, thoughts, breath,
and pot flower together.
The body sparkles with the flow
of fresh creek water splashing
over and around rocks,
everywhere reflecting trunk,
branch, leaves, and sky.
May all beings flower
in the brightness and clarity
of this heart working.

Acknowledgments

This book appears as the result of labors—known and unknown, re-membered and unremembered—and I know not how to offer my grati-tude for everyone's efforts, but I wish to thank a number of people in particular.

The Tassajara guest season recipes are from many sources. Each year a new set of guest cooks pick up where their predecessors left off. People experiment, dishes come and go. Some of the most recent guest cooks have been a particular help on this book. These include Jeffrey Schnei-der, Laurie Schley, Brian Fikes, Eleanor Edwards, Doug Volkmer, Brenda Grosz, Richard Jaffe, Elaine Maisner, and Jonathan Condit.

Many of our recipes have come to us by way of Greens, our restaurant in San Francisco, and the Tassajara Bread Bakery, our bakery there. We are especially indebted to Deborah Madison Welch and Jim Phalan for their remarkable contribution in creating and developing the Greens menu, for their unparalleled devotion and commitment to exploring and widening the range of what vegetarian cooking can be, and for car-ing—it makes all the difference.

Additionally, Deborah started this book, laboring several months, col-lecting recipes, reducing them to home scale and checking them. The book would not have happened without her.

At the bakery many people worked energetically and creatively. In particular, I would like to thank Peter Overton and Doug Volkmer for their many years of finding out what works for breads and pastries and for people.

My typists were also supportive, as well as hard-working: Liz Tuomi, Flora Taylor, Trish Crowell, Tara Thralls, and Myphon Hunt.

Several people looked over the manuscript. Martha Freebairn-Smith, Yvonne Rand, Patti Sullivan, Shirley Sarvis, Suzanne Simpson, and Mi-chael Sawyer all offered their encouragement and suggestions.

The book has been enriched with illustrations by Michael Sawyer and Eje Wray. I feel especially fortunate that Mayumi Oda was able to do a print for the cover.

Two long-time friends, my new neighbors, J.B. and Christine, have helped me through this time of transition in my life which has brought the book to fruition. The poet Rumi says, "We have ways within each other that can never be said by anyone." The ways of J.B. and Christine, however unsaid, have been healing and revitalizing, wondrous mid-wifery.

I would also like to point out and acknowledge that some of the recipes are adapted from other cookbooks, familiar to many of us. We all owe a great deal to the many people who have possessed not only an abiding interest in and passion for food, but also the skill—or audacity—to write down their collection of recipes. I want to thank them for their love of food and their painstaking efforts to share this love with others. Julia Child, Craig Claiborne, Elizabeth David, Marcela Hazan, Madhur Jaffrey, Madeleine Kammon, Diana Kennedy, Richard Olney, Irma Rombauer, Bill Shurtleff, and Alice Waters have all produced fine books about food and cooking. If I have omitted any of our "secret" sources, I apologize.

Personally, I have been nourished and inspired in recent years by the cooking at the restaurants of Alice Waters, Jeremiah Tower, Mark Miller, Patty Unterman, and Anne Powning, as well as at Greens.

Alive today are many deeply caring people who work hard, most often without recognition, to make a sustainable, nurturing, satisfying life we can pass on to future generations. May their efforts bear full, sweet fruit.

Autobiographical Tidbits

More than ten years have passed since my last cookbook, *Tassajara Cooking*, and fourteen years since *The Tassajara Bread Book*. Strange as it may seem, I write another cookbook now—not because I know more about cooking, but because I know something about writing cookbooks.

I have been fascinated by writing about food ever since I started reading M. F. K. Fisher when I was ten or eleven. *The Gastronomical Me, How to Cook a Wolf*: the titles alone had always attracted me, though I had no idea what "gastronomical" was or even how to pronounce it. (And I could not understand why anyone would write a whole book about cooking wolves when their meat was not available in the supermarket.) I read about a world in which food and cooking were integral to the fabric of daily life, not something to take time out for, to get out of the way, or just to fuel up on. Food was life. Life was food.

Still, I had always been intimidated at the prospect of cooking—until I started having dinner parties. Entering what appeared to be the mysterious, foreign, secret, complex, and demanding world of cooking, I soon realized that a cook just applies heat over time. Things cook.

I followed recipes and discovered that cooking was fun: the colors, shapes, aromas—an ever-changing canvas that only the cook can appreciate. And I enjoyed the companionship and conviviality. After a while, I looked in books less and started imagining more, daydreaming in flavors.

In 1967, I became the head cook at Tassajara Zen Mountain Center. I wanted to be famous, loved, and venerated. People mostly liked the food, but their liking did not seem to carry over to me. They said I was arrogant, bossy, short-tempered, and know-it-all. It took some convincing, but I finally had to admit I needed to work on myself, to work on how I worked and how I lived.

Over the years, when I have asked cooks at Zen Center what is the most difficult part about cooking, almost invariably the answer is: the people, having to work with others, having to work with yourself. The food takes care of itself.

So I remain convinced that the "best" cooking does not depend on anything more special than the willingness to do the work of putting yourself on the line, on the table. You get to know the ingredients, within and without, and how changeable they are, and put them together for everyone to see and, even more revealing, to taste.

The last ten years—a lot of water has gone under the bridge, and some bridges have gone under the water—I have spent studying, struggling, wrestling, wondering, "What is a spiritual life? What is a good life? How can we save ourselves, literally and spiritually?"

At the Zen Center in San Francisco, I have been guest manager, head of the meditation hall, head resident teacher, president, chairman of the board. (I find it a great irony: going to the mountains to attain true realization and becoming an executive officer in a huge "corporation.") At Greens, our restaurant in San Francisco, I have been busboy, dishwasher, waiter, host, cashier, floor manager, wine buyer, manager.

But none of this explains the real work. "My job," I've said in response to people's queries, "is to be happy. Others may be more naturally happy, but I have to work at it." It's good work and always available, though the pay is not always so great.

I want people to be happy. I want all beings to be happy. Not the happy of getting what you imagined wanting, but the happy of kind mind, joyful mind, big mind; the happy of a day of peace, a day of tending, of attending ("You have to be present to win!" Jack reminded us recently); the happy of being with, not being boss, of greeting, meeting, patience, warmth, generosity.

On a leave of absence from Zen Center, I am living in Inverness, California, cooking for friends and enjoying the woods.

November, 1984

WHO KNOWS WHAT THUS COMES?

Picking up an onion,
what is it held in hand?
How many dusty miles
and blazing asphalt truckstops,
hidden in darkness, locked in steel?
How many cups of coffee and tired-eyed
waitresses greeted the driver?
How many minutes of country music
and rambling thoughts helped onion here?
How many days at home, in ground,
intimately connected, embedded,
nestled unseen, rapt in absorption,
knowing just what to do
with earth and water, sun and wind,
to make them onion.
That everything thus comes
at once as onion, what
treasure is this dug up?
Who knows what hand holds?

Index

Notes